AF531382

Gandhi
Global
Series-1

MY LIFE

Creatively Illustrated to present his Real Life-Drama

Meet Munna Gandhi at age 7

INDIA BOOKVARSITY

LOTUS CHOICES

Editor: Mahendra Kulasrestha

Fresh Global Editions
for the Third Millenium

'A person like Buddha is born in India after 2000 years—in Gandhi.'
—**Gurudev Tagore**

'...the greatest person since Buddha... "'his great contribution was the theory and practice of non-violence...usage of moral weapons to achieve practical results.'
—**John Gunther**

'Gandhi belongs to tomorrow.'
—**Ralph Templin**

'It now remains for the people of india to take upon themselves Gandhi's world leadership for non-violence.'
—**Pearl Buck**

MY LIFE
In Search of Truth

An abridged version of
Gandhiji's Autobiography
for the general reader
worldwide

Mahatma Gandhi–as the World Knows

Gandhi Flowers

'To a starving person, God will appear in the form of bread alone.'

•

A Tid-bit

- *When Gandhi started his fast unto death in Yervada jail in 1932, Gurudev Tagore travelled the long distance and, sitting beside him on the cot, shed tears.*

The Inventor of Satyagraha

MY LIFE
IN SEARCH OF TRUTH
—M.K. Gandhi

Gandhi Global
New First Edition: 2016
ISBN: 978-81-8382-323-4

Published by:
Lotus Press Publishers & Distributors
Unit No. 220, IInd Floor, 4735/22, Prakash Deep Building,
Ansari Road, Darya Ganj, New Delhi-110002
Ph.: 23280047, 098118-38000 www.lotuspress.co.in
E-mail: lotuspress1984@gmail.com

Printed & Published by : **Lotus Press Publishers & Distributors,** New Delhi- 2

Editorspeak

•

Gandhi Global Series
Easy Reading for Every Home

Our motherland India s Gujarat-born son Mohandas Karamchand Gandhi, a bania by caste, and not a good looking person, has come to be regarded, as well as revered, by most, if not all, as the most important person public figure, political changemaker, saint in real life, originator of a new way of social togetherness, etc. of modern times. Much has been written about him and will continue to be written in times to come, because his work has the potential to control, guide and lead the conflict-ridden present day world, towards the fast developing process of globalisation, being the only effective way to reach it with minimum damage.

Without dilly-dallying left and right to present the theme in my mundane words, I ll immediately take recourse to Will Durant, the celebrated author of the 8-vol. Story of Civilisation and The Story of Philosophy of which 2.5 crore copies were sold in a dozen languages of the world a great favourite of the present writer also (inspired by which he edited and wrote a similar volume in Hindi, including Indian and Chinese thinkers) whose comments seem to be the best to me on the subject. Here goes:

> ...I honour Gandhi for his astonishing record of achievements:
>
> **First,** through leaping far ahead of the moral consciouness of mankind, which is yet tribal and national, he has helped the international organisation...for the larger morality in which the code of conduct between gentlemen will be applied to the conduct of nations.
>
> **Second,** he has lifted religion up to a plane where the most unscrupulons statesmen must reckon with it as a great force.
>
> **Third,** he has for a generation kept a great revolutionary movement from all but sporadic violence, he has refused to unleash the mob in this way he has been a boon to all humanity, which is so sensitive now to disorder anywhere. He has approached one of the fundamental principle of statesmanship: to persuade radicals that change must be gradual in order to be permanent, and to persuade the conservatives that change must be.
>
> **Fourth,** he has educated his people; he has aroused them, as no one before in their history, to the evils of untouchability, temple-prostitution, child-marriage, unmarrigeable widows, and the traffic in opium.
>
> **Fifth,** and despite his partial defence of that caste system which perpetually divides and weakens India, he has given to India a

psychological unity never possessed by it before, making all these races, languages and creeds feel and think alike, as the prelude to united action.

Sixth, he has given to his countrymen what they needed above everything else pride.

The unifier of India could not be a politician, he had to be a saint. Because Gandhi thought with his heart, India has followed him. The people of India do him reverence, and no man in the world weilds so great a spiritual influence.

Perhaps Gandhi will fail, as saints are likely to fail in this very Darwinian world. But how could we accept life if it did not, now and then, fling into the face of our successes some failure like that?*f*

Indians have come to be regarded as poor historians, to which I would like to add that we are worse promoters which, unfortunately, is the basic requirement for even right causes and which America is not, a significant reason for her great success. I once read in *Life* that would one believe it? one of the original founders of the nation, whose name I do not recall, was popularised by an artist by a portrait he made entirely on the basis of his fertile imagination. Similarly, the statue standing at the entry of Harvard University, does not illustrate the real person but the first person the sculptor met with in the morning when he decided to make one but did not find the real pic. Fine indeed!

We have so many Gandhi organiastions in the country, and about 120 large volumes of his Collected Work have been published by the government, but none has so far visualised a compendium of the Essential Gandhi for general use which can be placed in every home in India, and also in some enlightened homes abroad. We therefore have undertaken such a project in the present Gandhi Global Series of about half-a-dozen average-sized volumes on the major aspects of his life and work, suitably selected, edited and illustrated.

Insha-allah God-willing it is likely to include an abridged version of the very famous antobiography; his almost unknown commentary on the Gita which, in addition to his easy, even enjoyable, presentation, provides the most authentic insight into his own mind and value-system; two independent books on his major contributions to thought and public action: Ahimsa (Non-Violence) and Satyagraha (Passive Resistance); one or two containing select opinions of eminent men on his work, and a book of pithy quotations on the lines of the one which I once did for Nehru, selected by Rajiv when he was quite young. We intend to illustrate these with as many as possible of his photographs in action which reminds me of publishing in 1994 a total album of his photographs under the title Prophet of Peace , carried out as a project of Gandhi-Fuji Foundation for World Peace, of which I was the secretary but the Almighty did not make it succeed why, I ve yet to get an answer to. (That is why I ve invoked him in the beginning itself, hoping He ll be appeased.)

This also reminds me of another significant work I helped publish, Profiles of Gandhi , during the Gandhi centennial in 1968, an American project given to our publishing house Indian Book Company; edited by the well known Norman Cousins, a large-sized profusely illustrated work, and contributed by celebrities like Will Durant, Louis Fischer, Margaret Sanger, Margaret Burke-White, John Gunther, etc., etc., etc., a remarkable work on the subject, a tribute par excellence.

As I conclude this note on this unexpectedly balmy morning of 30 Sept. 2013, I find in the *Times of India* the release of Prakash Jha s new film Satyagraha given 4^ stars by its critic taking up the current issue of corruption Amitabh Bachchan going on hunger strike; is Gandhi returning?

There seems to be a glimpse of Gandhi in the new Anna Hazare movement, too though it does not seem to be bothering the Sonia Gandhi-led central government. The new national slogan that has come up, is:

Aam Aadmi kitna aam,

Raghupati Raghav Raja Ram.

There are 127 crores of AAM aadmis in India now to be taken care of. And the numbers are fast increasing.

Amen!

Gandhi Flowers

'Prayer needs a heart, not a tongue;
Without the heart,
Words have no meaning.'

•

A Tid-bit

• *At the second Round-Table Conference held in London in 1931, Gandhi was the only person representing the Congress, while the Hindu Mahasabha was present with a large delegation, headed by Dr. B.B. Munje. On their return to India, they gathered in Pune to discuss; Dr. Munje stated that nobody paid any attention to anybody other than Gandhi; so they couldn't do anything worthwhile.*

Einstein on Gandhi

•

Greatest Political Genius of Our Time

The veneration in which Gandhi has been held throughout the world rests on the recognition, for the most part unconscious, that in our age of moral decay, he was the only statesman who represented that higher conception of human relations in the political sphere to which we must aspire with all our powers. We must learn the difficult lesson that the future of mankind will only be tolerable when our course, in world affairs as in all other matters, is based upon justice and law rather than the threat of naked power, as has been true so far.

Gandhi, the greatest political genius of our time, indicated the path to be taken. He gave proof of what sacrifice man is capable of once he has discovered the right path. His work on behalf of India s liberation is living testimony to the fact that man s will, sustained by an indomitable conviction, is more powerful than material forces that seem insurmountable.

On the whole I believe that Gandhi held the

most enlightened views of the political men in our times. We should strive to do things in the spirit not to use violence in fighting for our case and to refrain from taking part in anything we believe as evil.

Revolution, without the use of violence, was the method by which Gandhi brought about the liberation of India. It is my belief that the problem of bringing peace to the world on a supranational basis will be solved only by employing Gandhi s method on a large scale.

I have been pacifist all my life and regard Gandhi as the only truly great political figure of our age. Generations to come will scarce believe that such a one as this even in flesh and blood walked upon the earth.

New

Remember Ho Chi Minh?

Yes, the famous liberation warrior of Viet Nam of the older generation.

The new Hindi fortnightly Yathavat , edited by Ram Bahadur Rai, in its 16-31 Oct. 2013 issue, in a well-written article on communism in India, by Shiv Kumar Mishra, states that a former communist M.P., A.K. Damodaran, once told him that **Ho Chi Minh had told him that he regarded himself as Gandhi s disciple.**

Hurrah!

Contents

•

Gandhi Flowers

'Faith that never varies, but waxes bright, turns in to realisation.'

•

A Tid-bit

- *M.A. Jinnah was President of Home Rule League in Bombay, when members, influenced by Gandhi's popularity, wanted to offer him the position. Jinnah agreed, but commented that he'll change the society's name. Which he promptly did, renaming it as Swaraj Sabha.*

WELCOME
TO
'MY LIFE'

Gandhi Flowers

'He who always treads on the path of truth, never trembles.'

•

'His greatness lay in doing what everybody could but doesn't .'

—Louis Fischer

1
MY BOYHOOD
From Birth till Age 18

The Gandhis belong to the Bania caste. But from my grandfather, they have been Prime Ministers in several Kathiawad states. Karamchand Gandhi, *alias* Kaba Gandhi, and Tulsidas Gandhi were Prime Ministers in Porbandar, one after the other. Kaba Gandhi was my father. He was a member of the Rajasthanik Court. Kaba Gandhi married four times in succession, having lost his wife each time by death. His last wife, Putlibai, bore him a daughter and three sons, I being the youngest.

I must have been about seven when my father left Porbandar for Rajkot to become a member of the Rajasthanik Court. There I was put into a primary school, and there is hardly anything to note about my studies. **I could only have been a mediocre student.** From this school I went to the suburban school and then to the high school. I do not remember having ever told a lie, during this short period, either to my teachers or to my schoolmates. I used to be very shy and avoided all company. To be at school at the stroke of the hour and to run back home as soon as the school closed that was my daily habit. I literally ran back, because I could not bear to talk to anybody. I was even afraid lest anyone should poke fun at me.

There is an incident which occurred at the examination during my first year at the high school. Mr. Giles, the Educational Inspector, had come on a visit of inspection. He had set us five words to write as a spelling exercise. One of the words was kettle . I had misspelt it. **The teacher tried to prompt me with the point of his boot, but I would not be prompted.** It was beyond me to see that he wanted me to copy the spelling from my neighbour s slate, for I had thought that the teacher was there to supervise us against copying. The result was that all the boys, except myself, were found to have spelt every word correctly. Only I had been stupid. The teacher tried later to bring this stupidity home to me, but without effect. I never could learn the art of copying .

We were three brothers. The first was already married. The elders decided to marry my second brother, who was two or three years my senior, a cousin, possibly a year older, and me, all at the same time. I do not think it meant to me anything more than the prospect of good clothes to wear, drum-beating, marriage processions, rich dinners and a strange girl to play with. I can picture to myself, even today, how we sat on our wedding dais, how we performed the Saptapadi, how we, the newly wedded husband and wife, put the sweet Kansar into each other s mouth, and how we began to live together, and oh! that first night. Two innocent

Meet Lallu Gandhi at age 14 — looks a little too serious

'India is essentially
karmabhumi (land of duty)
in contradistinction to
bhogabhumi (land of enjoyment)'.

'Of all the revolutionaries of the century– Lenin, Mussolini, Mao, etc. —Gandhi alone offered hope for reform without distruction.'

—***Chester Bowles***

Meet Sona Gandhi—
handsome and westernised,
in England

'For me
patriotism is the same as humanity,
I am patriotic
because
I am human and humane.
It is not exclusive.'

'He was one of those prophets who
lived far ahead of his times.'

—***Gen. MacArthur***

Meet Advocate Gandhi—
Matric, Bar-at-Law,
Middle Temple,

'The word Swaraj is a sacred word,
a Vedic word
meaning self-rule and self-restraint
and
no freedom from all restraints
which 'independence' often means.'

'Gandhi was a devoted Hindu, and
a philosophic Hindu can be at home
with many religions, as he notably
proved!'

—Norman Thomas

Meet Magic Gandhi
in London
—as he attended
the Round Table
Conference

Wow! What a Change!

'You can chain me
you can torture me,
you can even destroy this body,
but you will never
imprison my mind.'

'Gandhi died by violence, because he
was staking his life in order
to set the example of non-violence!'

—***Walter Lippman***

children all unwittingly hurled themselves into the ocean of life. My brother s wife had thoroughly coached me about my behaviour on the first night.

Kasturbai was illiterate. By nature she was simple, independent, persevering and, with me at least, reticent. My passion was entirely centred on one woman, and I wanted it to be reciprocated. **I was passionately fond of her. Even at school I used to think of her, and the thought of nightfall and our subsequent meeting was ever haunting me. Separation was unbearable. I used to keep her awake till late in the night with my idle talk.**

I was very anxious to teach her, but lustful love left me no time. For one thing, the teaching had to be done against her will, and that too at night. I dared not meet her in the presence of the elders, much less talk to her. I failed likewise to instruct her through private tutors. As a result Kasturbai can now with difficulty write simple letters and understand simple Gujarati.

During the first five years of our married life (from the age of 13 to 18), we could not have lived together longer than an aggregate period of three years. **At the age of eighteen I went to England.** I was learning at the high school when I was married. I was not regarded as a dunce at the high school. I always enjoyed the affection of my teachers. I never had a bad certificate. In fact I even won prizes after I passed out of the second standard. In the fifth and sixth I obtained scholarships of rupees four and ten respectively, an achievement for which I have to thank good luck more than my merit.

I had not any high regard for my ability. I used to be astonished whenever I won prizes and scholarships. But I very jealously guarded my character. The least little blemish drew tears from my eyes. I once received corporal punishment. I did not so much mind the punishment, as the fact that it was considered my desert. I wept piteously. That was when I was in the first or second standard. **I never took part in any exercise, cricket or football, before they were made compulsory.** My shyness was one of the reasons for this aloofness.

Eating Meat

Amongst my few friends at the high school I had, at different times, two who might be called intimate. One of these friendships did not last long. He forsook me, because I made friends with the other. A wave of reform was sweeping over Rajkot at the time when I first came across this friend. He informed me that many of our teachers were secretly taking meat and wine. He also named many well-known people of Rajkot as belonging to the same company. There were also, I was told, some high school boys among them.

I was surprised and pained. I asked my friend the reason and he explained it thus: **We are a weak people because we do not eat meat. The English are able to rule over us, because they are meateaters.** You know how hardy I am, and how great a runner, too. It is because I am a meateater. There is nothing like trying.

A day was thereupon fixed for beginning the experiment. It had to be conducted in secret. The

Gandhis were Vaishnavas. I was extremely devoted to my parents. I knew that the moment they came to know of my having eaten meat, they would be shocked to death. I wished to be strong and daring and wanted my countrymen also to be such, so that we might defeat the English and make India free.

So the day came. We went in search of a lonely spot by the river, and there I saw, for the first time in my life meat. There was baker s bread also. I relished neither. **The goat s meat was as tough as leather. I simply could not eat it.** I was sick. I had a very bad night afterwards.

My friend was not a man to give in easily. He now began to cook various delicacies with meat and dress them neatly. And for dining, a State house, with its dining hall, and tables and chairs, about which my friend had made arrangements in collusion with the chief cook there. This bait had its effect. **I got over my dislike for bread, forswore my compassion for the goats, and became a relisher of meat-dishes.**

This went on for about a year. But not more than half a dozen meat-feasts were enjoyed in all; because the State house was not available every day. I had no money to pay for this reform . My friend had therefore always to find the wherewithal. Whenever I had occasion to indulge in these surreptitious feasts, dinner at home was out of the question. My mother would naturally ask me and want to know the reason why I did not wish to eat. I would say to her, I have no appetite today; there is something wrong with my digestion.

I knew I was lying. Therefore I said to myself: Though it is essential to eat meat, and also essential to take up food reform in the country, yet **deceiving and lying to one s father and mother is worse than not eating meat. When they are no more and I have found my freedom, I will eat meat openly.** This decision I communicated to my friend, and I have never since gone back to it.

Visiting a Brothel

The same company would have led me into faithlessness to my wife. But I was saved by the skin of my teeth. My friend once took me to a brothel. He sent me in with the necessary instructions. It was all prearranged. The bill had already been paid. I went into the jaws of sin, but God in His infinite mercy protected me against myself. **I was almost struck blind and dumb in this den of vice. I sat near the woman on her bed, but I was tongue-tied. She naturally lost patience with me, and showed me the door, with abuses and insults.**

I can recall four more similar incidents in my life, and in most of them my good fortune, rather than any effort on my part, saved me.

Smoking, Stealing Gold....

A relative and I became fond of smoking. My uncle had the habit and when we saw him smoking, we thought we should copy his example. But we had no money. So **we began pilfering stumps of cigarettes thrown away by my uncle.** The stumps, however, were not always available, and could not emit much smoke either. So **we began to steal coins from the servant s pocket money in order**

to purchase Indian cigarettes (*bidis*). But the question was where to keep them. We managed somehow for a few weeks on these stolen coins. In the meantime we heard that the stalks of a certain plant were porous and could be smoked like cigarettes. We got them and began this kind of smoking.

But we were far from being satisfied with such things as these. Our want of independence began to smart. It was unbearable that we should be unable to do anything without the elders permission. At last, **in sheer disgust, we decided to commit suicide!** But how were we to do it? From where were we to get the poison? We heard that Dhatura seeds were an effective poison. Off we went to the jungle in search of these seeds, and got them. We went to Kedarji Mandir, put ghee in the temple-lamp, had the *darshan* and then looked for a lonely corner.

But our courage failed us. Supposing we were not instantly killed? Why not rather put up with the lack of independence? But we swallowed two or three seeds nevertheless. We dared not take more. Both of us fought shy of death, and decided to go to Ramji Mandir to compose ourselves, and to dismiss the thought of suicide.

But much more serious than this theft was the one I was guilty of a little later. I pilfered the coins when I was twelve or thirteen. The other theft was committed when I was fifteen. In this case **I stole a bit of gold out of my meateating brother s armlet.** But this became more than I could bear. I resolved never to steal again. I also made up my mind to confess it to my father. I decided to write out the confession, to submit it to my father, and ask his forgiveness. I wrote it on a slip of paper and handed it to him myself.

I was trembling as I handed the confession to my father. He was then suffering from fistula and was confined to bed. He read it through, and pearl-drops trickled down his cheeks, wetting the paper. I could see my father s agony. Those pearl-drops of love cleansed my heart, and washed my sin away.

This was for me an object lesson in Ahimsa. Then I could read in it nothing more than a father s love, but today I know that it was pure Ahimsa. When such Ahimsa becomes all-embracing, it transforms everything it touches. There is no limit to its power.

The time of which I am now speaking is my sixteenth year. My father was bed-ridden, I had the duties of a nurse, which mainly consisted in dressing the wound, giving my father his medicine, and compounding drugs whenever they had to be made up at home. Every night I massaged his legs and retired only when he asked me to do so or after he had fallen asleep.

This was also the time when my wife was expecting a baby a circumstance which, as I can see today, meant a double shame for me. For one thing, I did not restrain myself, as I should have done, whilst I was yet a student. And secondly, my devotion to my parents, Shravana having been my

*Meet Barrister Gandhi
in S. Africa*

'Not to have control over the senses
is like sailing in a
rudderless ship
bound to break to pieces
on coming in contact with
the very first rock.'

'I know Gandhi spoke of the convictions of the American people as clearly as he spoke for Indian.'

—*President Eisenhower*

Meet Neta Gandhi in S. Africa,
with Kasturbai—
towards becoming GANDHI

'Khadi to me
is the symbol of
unity of Indian humanity,
of its
economic freedom
and equality.'

'The light of Mohandas K. Gandhi
turns brightly as it became for Indians,
for Americans and for all the world.'

—President Lyndon B. Johnson

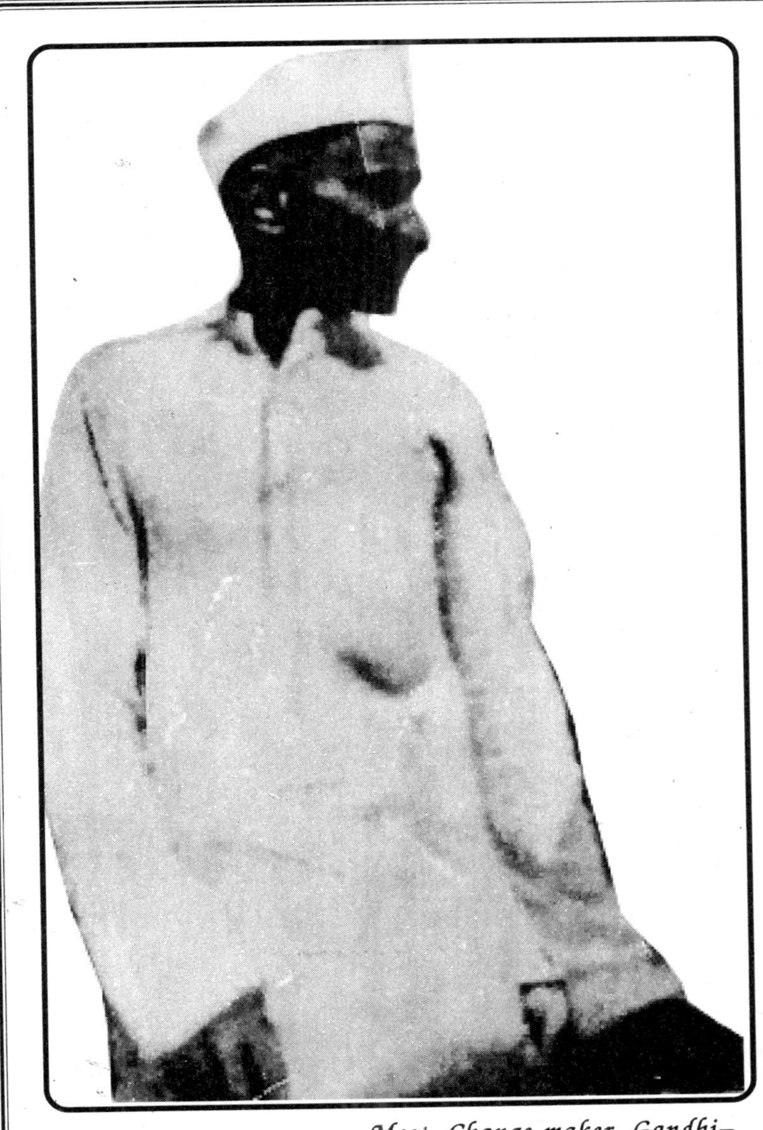

Meet Change-maker Gandhi–
In khadi cap, which became
the symbol of India's freedom

'My Ahimsa would not tolerate
the idea of
giving a free meal to
a healthy person who
has not worked for it in
some honest way.'

'Gandhi was a leader of international stature. His actions have left a deep impression on millions of people.'

—*President Truman*

*Meet Economist Gandhi–
with Charkha, to start the
Swadeshi movement*

'Non-violence in its dynamic condition
means conscious suffering.
It does not mean meek submission
to
the will of
the evildoer,
but it means
pitting of one's whole soul
against
the will of the tyrant.'

'Gandhi's philosophy postulates a
universe very different from that
governed by the law of the fish.'

—*Charles Drekmeter*

ideal since childhood. Every night whilst my hands were busy massaging my father s legs, my mind was hovering about the bed-room.

The dreadful night came. It was 10-30 or 11 p.m. I was giving the massage. My uncle offered to relieve me. I was glad and went straight to the bed-room. My wife, poor thing, was fast asleep. I woke her up. In five or six minutes, however, the servant knocked at the door. I started with alarm. Get up, he said. Father is very ill. I sprang out of bed.

'What is the matter? Do tell me!

'Father is no more.'

I had but to wring my hands. I felt deeply ashamed and miserable. I ran to my father s room. I saw that **if animal passion had not blinded me, I should have been spared the torture of separation from my father during his last moments.** I should have been massaging him, and he would have died in my arms. But now it was my uncle who had this privilege.

Entry into Religion

Being born in the Vaishnava faith, I had often to go to the temple, called Haveli. But it never appealed to me. I did not like its glitter and pomp. Also I heard rumours of immorality being practised there, and lost all interest in it.

But what I failed to get there I obtained from my nurse, an old servant of the family. There was in me a fear of ghosts and spirits. Rambha, for that was her name, suggested, as a remedy for this fear, the repetition of Ramanama. So at a tender age I began repeating Ramanama to cure my fear of ghosts and spirits. This was, of course, shortlived, but the good seed sown in childhood was not sown in vain. **Today Ramanama is an infallible remedy for me.**

A few months after this we came to Rajkot. The *Bhagavat* used to be read on every Ekadashi day. Sometimes I attended the reading. In Rajkot, however, I got an early grounding in toleration for all branches of Hinduism and sister religions. For my father and mother I would visit the Haveli as also Shiva s and Rama s temples, who would take or send us youngsters there. Jain monks also would pay frequent visits to my father.

He had, besides, Muslim and Parsi friends, who would talk to him about their own faiths, and he would listen to them always with respect, and often with interest. **These many things combined to inculcate in me a toleration for all faiths.** Only Christianity was at the time an exception. I developed a sort of dislike for it. And for a reason. In those days **Christian missionaries used to stand in a corner near the high school and hold forth, pouring abuse on Hindus and their gods. I could not endure this.** I heard of a well-known Hindu having been converted to Christianity. It was the talk of the town that, when he was baptized, he had to eat beef and drink liquor, that he also had to change his clothes. These things got on my nerves. Surely, thought I, a religion that compelled one to eat beef, drink liquor, and change one s own clothes did not deserve the name. I also heard that the new convert had already begun abusing the religion of his ancestors, their customs and their country. All these things created in me a dislike for Christianity.

◆◆◆

Gandhi Flowers

'When the ego dies, the soul awakens. When the soul awakens, all sorrows vanish.'

●

2
STUDIES IN ENGLAND
Age 18-21

I passed the matriculation examination in 1887. My elders wanted me to pursue my studies at college. There was a college in Bhavnagar as well as in Bombay, and as the former was cheaper, **I decided to go there and join the Samaldas College. I went, but found myself entirely at sea.** Everything was difficult. I could not follow, let alone taking interest in, the professors lectures. **At the end of the first term, I returned home.**

Bar at-Law Very Easy

We had in Mavji Dave an old friend and adviser of the family. Learning that I was at Samaldas College, he said: The times are changed. And none of you can expect to succeed to your father s position without having had a proper education. Now as this boy is still pursuing his studies, you should all look to him to keep it. It will take him four or five years to get his B.A. degree, which will at best qualify him for a sixty rupees post, not for a Diwanship. If like my son he went in for law, it would take him still longer. I would far rather that you sent him to England. **My son Kevalram says it is very easy**

to become a barrister. In three years time he will return. Also expenses will not exceed four to five thousand rupees. **I would strongly advise you to send Mohandas to England this very year.**

My elder brother was greatly exercised in his mind. How was he to find the wherewithal to send me? My mother was sorely perplexed. She did not like the idea of parting with me. My brother had another idea. He said to me: We have a certain claim on the Porbandar State. Mr. Lely is the Administrator. He thinks highly of our family and Uncle is in his good books. It is just possible that he might recommend you for some State help for your education in England.

I liked all this and got ready to start off for Porbandar. **There was no railway in those days. It was a five days bullock-cart journey. I hired a bullock-cart as far as Dhoraji, and from Dhoraji I took a camel in order to get to Porbandar a day quicker.**

I wrote to Mr. Lely, who asked me to see him at his residence. He saw me as he was ascending the staircase; and saying curtly, Pass your B.A. first and then see me. No help can be given to you now,' he hurried upstairs. I had made elaborate preparations to meet him. I had carefully learnt up a few sentences and had bowed low and saluted him with both hands. But all to no purpose!

I returned to Rajkot and reported all that had happened. I consulted Joshiji, who of course advised even incurring a debt if necessary. I suggested the disposal of my wife s ornaments, which could fetch about two to three thousand rupees. My brother promised to find the money somehow. My mother, however, was still unwilling. Someone had told her that young men got lost in England. Someone else had said that they took to meat and yet another that they could not live there without liquor. How about all this? she asked me. I said: Will you not trust me? I shall not lie to you. I swear that I shall not touch any of those things. But how can I trust you in a distant land? I will ask Becharji Swami.

Becharji Swami was a family adviser like Joshiji. He came to my help, and said: I shall get the boy solemnly to take the three vows, and then he can be allowed to go. He administered the oath and **I vowed not to touch wine, woman and meat.** This done, my mother gave her permission. With the blessings of my elders, I started for Bombay.

Meanwhile, my caste-people were agitated over my going abroad. A general meeting of the caste was called and I was summoned to appear before it. The Sheth the headman of the community thus accosted me: In the opinion of the caste, your proposal to go to England is not proper. Our religion forbids voyages abroad. We have also heard that it is not possible to live there without compromising our religion. One is obliged to eat and drink with Europeans!

To which I replied: I do not think it is at all against our religion to go to England. I intend going there for further studies. And I have already solemnly promised to my mother to abstain from

In S. Africa during the Boer war—Gandhi at 30 organised an Ambulance Corps of 1100 persons — and became Sergeant-Major.

'Realization of the goal
is in exact proportion to
that of the means.
This is a proposition that admits
of no exception.'

'From my background, I gained
my regulating Christian ideals,
from Gandhi I learned my
operational techique.'

—Martin Luther King

In S. Africa Gandhi founded the Phoenix Settlement to experiment in self-sufficient community living

'My patriotism is both
exclusive and inclusive.
It is exclusive in the sense that in all
humility I confine my attention to the
land of my birth;
But is inclusive in the sense
that my service is not
of a competitive or antoginistic
nature.'

'Gandhi believed in non-violence as an
end, and not just a means...
he forged his mighty weapon in
a life-long quest for peace in
his own soul.'

*—Editorial, Life
Magazine, 1965*

Gandhi (Sitting, centre) with members of Anglo-Indian Association, Transvaal

'Truth quenches untruth,
love quenches anger,
Self-suffering quenches violence;
This eternal rule
is a rule not for saints only
but for all.'

'In Gandhi's teachings and writings, I think you'll find no lies, no meanness, no slander, no dogmatism, no hypocrisy, no fear, no arrogance, no false pride, no hatred, no claims of infallibility...'

—*Edgar P. Snow*

At the Round Table Conference, London, 1931

Young men claiming to be
the fathers of tomorrow
should be the salt of the nation.
If
the salt loses its flavour
wherewith shall it
be salted?'

'There has never been anybody
quite like the Mahatma...When he
was needed, he came as a new creation,
straight from the hand of God.'

—John Haynes Holmes

With Sardar Patel, at Congress Session

'Mass illiteracy is India's
sin and shame and
must be liquidated.
The literacy campaign
must not begin and end
with a knowledge of the alphabet;
it must go hand in hand
with the spread
of useful knowledge.'

'Gandhi's influence has been
immense—beginning with Louis
Fischer, who was dogmatically
a pro-communist writer,
until he delved into
Gandhi's creed.'

—***Sydney Harris***

three things you fear most. I am sure the vow will keep me safe.

But we tell you, rejoined the Sheth, that it is *not* possible to keep our religion there. You know my relations with your father and you ought to listen to my advice.

I am really helpless. I think the caste should not interfere in the matter.

This incensed the Sheth. He swore at me. I sat unmoved. So the Sheth pronounced his order: **This boy shall be treated as an outcaste from today**. Whoever helps him or goes to see him off at the dock shall be punishable with a fine of one rupee four annas.

The order had no effect on me, and I took my leave of the Sheth. I sailed at last from Bombay on the 4th of September.

In London

I reached Southampton on a Saturday. On the boat I had worn a black suit, the white flannel one, kept especially for wearing when I landed. Those were the last days of September, and I found I was the only person wearing such clothes.

I had four notes of introduction: to Dr. P. J. Mehta, to Sjt. Dalpatram Shukla, to Prince Ranjitsinhji and to **Dadabhai Naoroji**. Someone on board had advised us to put up at the Victoria Hotel in London. Sjt. Mazmudar and I accordingly went there.

Dr. Mehta, to whom I had wired from Southampton, called at about eight o clock the same evening. As we were talking, I casually picked up his top-hat, and trying to see how smooth it was, passed my hand over it the wrong way and disturbed the fur. Dr. Mehta looked somewhat angrily at what I was doing and stopped me. **The incident was a warning for the future. This was my first lesson in European etiquette,** into the details of which Dr. Mehta humorously initiated me: 'Do not touch other people s things, he said. Do not ask questions as we usually do in India on first acquaintance; do not talk loudly. And so on and so forth. He also told me that it was very expensive to live in a hotel and recommended that I should live with a private family.

On Monday, we paid up our bills and went to the rooms rented for us; my hotel bill came to £ 3, an amount which shocked me. And I had practically starved in spite of this heavy bill!

I was very uneasy even in the new rooms. I would continually think of my home and country. My mother s love always haunted me. At night the tears would stream down my cheeks. Everything was strange the people, their ways, and even their dwellings. There was the additional inconvenience of the vegetarian vow. England I could not bear, but to return to India was not to be thought of. Now that I had come, I must finish the three years, said the inner voice.

Dr. Mehta went on Monday to Victoria Hotel expecting to find me there. He discovered that we had left, got our new address, and met me at our rooms. Dr. Mehta inspected my room and its appointments and shook his head in disapproval. This place won t do, he said. We come to England not so much for the purpose of studies as for gaining experience of English life and customs. And for this you need to live with a family. But before you do so, I think you had better serve a period of apprenticeship with ... I will take you there.

I gratefully accepted the suggestion and moved to the friend s rooms. He was all kindness and attention. He treated me as his own brother, initiated me into English ways and manners, and accustomed me to talking the language. My food, however, became a serious question. The landlady was at a loss to know what to prepare for me. The friend continually reasoned with me to eat meat, but I always pleaded my vow and then remained silent. The friend once got disgusted with this state of things, and said: Had you been my own brother, I would have sent you packing. What is the value of a vow made before an illiterate mother, and in ignorance of conditions here?

But I was adamant.

The friend s house was in Richmond, and it was not possible to go to London more than once or twice a week. Dr. Mehta and Sjt. Dalpatram Shukla therefore decided that I should be put with some family. Sjt. Shukla hit upon an Anglo-Indian s house in West Kensington and placed me there. The landlady was a widow. Here too I practically had to starve. I had sent for sweets and other eatables from home, but nothing had yet come. I was still as shy as ever and dared not ask for more than was put before me. She had two daughters. They insisted on serving me with an extra slice or two of bread. But little did they know that nothing less than a loaf would have filled me.

But I had found my feet now. I had not yet started upon my regular studies. I had just begun reading newspapers. I launched out in search of a vegetarian restaurant. **I would trot ten or twelve miles each day, go into a cheap restaurant and eat my fill of bread**, but would never be satisfied. I once hit on a vegetarian restaurant in Farringdon Street. The sight of it filled me with joy I noticed books for sale exhibited under a glass window near the door. I saw among them Salt s *A Plea for Vegetarianism.* This I purchased for a shilling and went straight to the dining room. This was my first hearty meal since my arrival in England.

Dance and Violin

Meanwhile, my friend had not ceased to worry about me. He one day invited me to go to the theatre. Before the play we were to dine together at the Holborn Restaurant, to me a palatial place. The friend had planned to take me to this restaurant evidently imagining that modesty would forbid any questions. The first course was soup. I wondered what it might be made of, but dare not ask the friend about it. I therefore summoned the waiter. My friend saw the movement and sternly asked across the table what was the matter. You are too clumsy for decent society, he passionately exclaimed. If you cannot behave yourself, you had better go. Feed in some other restaurant and await me outside. This delighted me. Out I went. There was a vegetarian restaurant close by, but it was closed. So I went without food that night. But I decided that I should assure him that I would be clumsy no more, but try to become polished. And for this purpose I undertook the all too impossible task of becoming an English gentleman.

The clothes after the Bombay cut that I was wearing were, I thought, unsuitable for English society, and I got new ones at the Army and Navy Stores. I also went in for a chimney-pot hat costing ninteen shillings I wasted ten pounds on an evening suit made in Bond Street, and got my good and noble-hearted brother to send me a double watch-chain of gold. It was not correct to wear a ready-made tie and I learnt the art of tying one for myself. **I wasted ten minutes every day before a huge mirror, watching myself arranging my tie and parting my hair in the correct fashion**. My hair was by no means soft, and every day it meant a regular struggle with the brush to keep it in position.

I was told it was necessary for me to take lessons in dancing, French and elocution. I decided to take dancing lessons at a class and paid down £ 3 as fees for a term. I must have taken about six lessons in three weeks. But it was beyond me to achieve anything like rhythmic motion. What then was I to do? I thought I should learn to play the violin, so I invested £ 3 in a violin and something more in fees.

I sought a third teacher to give me lessons in elocution and paid him a preliminary fee of a guinea.

I had not to spend a lifetime in England, I said to myself. I was a student and ought to go on with my studies. I should qualify myself to join the Inns Court. These and similar thoughts possessed me, and I expressed them in a letter which I addressed to the elocution teacher, requesting him to excuse me from further lessons. I wrote a similar letter to the dancing teacher, and went personally to the violin teacher with a request to dispose of the violin for any price it might fetch. She was rather friendly to me, so I told her how I had discovered that I was pursuing a false idea. She encouraged me in the determination to make a complete change. This infatuation must have lasted about three months. **The punctiliousness in dress persisted for years. But henceforward I became a student.**

London Matriculation

So I decided to take rooms on my own account. The rooms were so selected as to enable me to reach the place of business on foot in half an hour, and so save fares. The new arrangement combined walks and economy, as it meant a saving of fares and gave me walks of eight or ten miles a day. It was mainly this habit of long walks that kept me practically free from illness throughout my stay in England and gave me a fairly strong body.

I knew that Bar examinations did not require much study, and I therefore did not feel pressed for time. **My weak English was a perpetual worry**

to me. I should, I thought, not only be called to the Bar, but have some literary degree as well. A friend suggested that I should pass the London Matriculation. But the syllabus frightened me. Latin and a modern language were compulsory. But the friend entered a strong plea for it: Latin is very valuable to lawyers. Knowledge of Latin is very useful in understanding law-books. And one paper in Roman Law is entirely in Latin. I decided to learn Latin, no matter how difficult it might be. French I had already begun, so I thought that it should be the modern language.

I joined a private Matriculation class. Examinations were held every six months and I had only five months at my disposal. I framed my own time-table to the minute; but neither my intelligence nor memory promised to enable me to tackle Latin and French besides subjects within the given period. The result was that I failed in Latin. I was sorry but did not lose heart.

I made an effort to simplify my life still further. I came across a fair number of poor students living more humbly than I. One of them was staying in the slums in a room at two shillings a week and living on two pence worth of cocoa and bread per meal from Lockhart s cheap Cocoa Rooms. It was far from me to think of emulating him, but I felt I could surely have one room instead of two and cook some of my meals at home. That would be a saving of four to five pounds each month.

I gave up the suite of rooms and rented one instead, invested in a stove, and began cooking my breakfast at home. I had lunch out and for dinner, bread and cocoa at home. Thus I managed to live on a shilling and three pence a day. This was also a period of intensive study. Plain living saved me plenty of time and I passed my examination.

There was a Vegetarian Society in England with a weekly journal of its own. I subscribed to the weekly, joined the Society and very shortly found myself on its Executive Committee. Here I came in contact with those who were regarded as pillars of vegetarianism, and began my own experiments in dietetics. I stopped taking the sweets and condiments I had got from home. And I now relished the boiled spinach cooked without condiments.

Full of the neophyte's zeal for vegetarianism, I decided to start a vegetarian club in my locality, Bayswater. I invited **Sir Edwin Arnold,** who lived there, to be Vice-President. Dr. Oldfield who was Editor of *The Vegetarian* became President. I myself became the Secretary. I was elected to the Executive Committee of the Vegetarian Society, and made it a point to attend everyone of its meetings, but I always felt tongue-tied. Dr. Oldfield once said to me, You talk to me quite all right, but why is it that you never open your lips at a committee meeting? **Not that I never felt tempted to speak, but I was at a loss now to how to express myself.** This went on for a long time.

Meantime, a serious question came up for discussion. I thought it wrong to be absent, and felt it cowardice to register a silent vote. The President of the Society was Mr. Hills, and the existence of the Society depended practically on his financial assistance. Dr. Allinson was an advocate of the then new birth control movement. Mr. Hills regarded these methods as cutting at the root of morals. And that a man of Dr. Allinson s views should not be allowed to remain in the Society. A motion was therefore brought for his removal.

The question deeply interested me. But I thought it was quite improper to exclude a man from a vegetarian society simply because he refused to regard puritan morals as one of the objects of the Society. I felt myself personally called upon to express my own. How to do it was the question. I had not the courage to speak and I therefore decided to set down my thoughts in writing. **I went to the meeting with the document in my pocket. So far as I recollect, I did not find myself equal even to reading it, and the president had it read by someone else. This shyness I retained throughout my stay in England.**

I once went to Ventnor with Sjt. Mazmudar. We stayed there with a vegetarian family. Mr. Howard, the author of *The Ethics of Diet,* was also staying at the same watering-place. We met him, and he invited us to speak at a meeting for the promotion of vegetarianism. I had ascertained that it was not considered incorrect to read one s speech. To speak extempore would have been out of the question for me. **I had therefore written down my speech. I stood up to read it, but could not. My vision became blurred and I trembled**. Sjt. Mazmudar had to read it for me.

My last effort to make a public speech in England was on the eve of my departure for home. I invited my vegetarian friends to dinner in the Holborn Restaurant. Speeches there had to be. When my turn for speaking came, **I stood up to make a speech. I had with great care thought out one which would consist of a very few sentences. But I could not proceed beyond the first sentence.** I thank you, gentlemen, for having kindly responded to my invitation, I said abruptly, and sat down.

Trying to Pass Off as a Bachelor

There were comparatively few Indian students in England at that time. It was a practice with them to affect the bachelor even though they might be married. School or college students in England are all bachelors, studies being regarded as incompatible with married life. Indian youths in England, therefore, felt ashamed to confess that they were married. There was also another reason, that in the event of the fact being known it would be impossible for the young men to go about or flirt with the young girls of the family in which they lived.

I too caught the contagion. I did not hesitate to pass myself off as a bachelor though I was married and father of a son. Only my reserve and my reticence saved me. It was customary in families like the one in which I was staying at Ventnor, for the daughter of the landlady to take out guests for a walk. My landlady s daughter took me one day to the lovely hills round Ventnor. I was no slow walker,

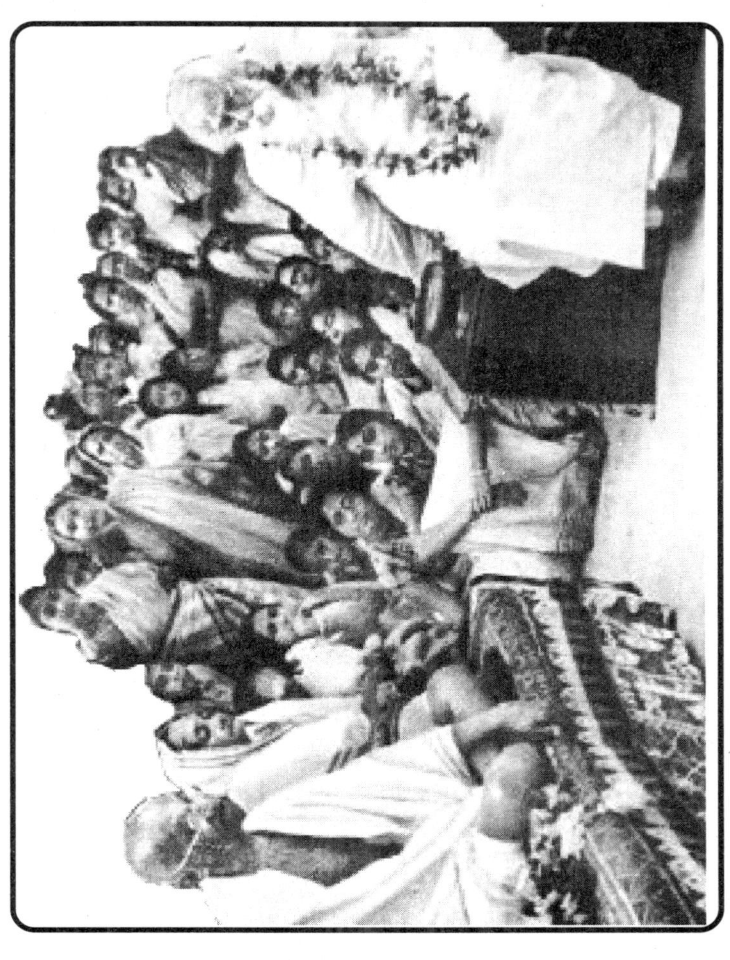

With Rabindranath Tagore at Santiniketan

'Our children must
from their infancy
be taught the dignity of labour.'

'Gandhi spent over 2000 days in
prisons, reading, meditating, and
drove the British frantic with his final,
bloodless weapon: fasting.'

—***Leo Rosten***

Leading the famous Salt March

'Culture of the mind
must be subservient
to the heart.'

'...the bare little room that
Gandhi used ... and I stood at
the entrance awed by the thought
of the power of the man who had lived
there. All there was—a rug, a rolled up
pad that he used at night, as pillow.'

—*Eleanor Roosevelt*

but my companion walked even faster, dragging me after her and chattering away all the while. I responded to her chatter sometimes with a whispered yes or no , or at the most. Yes, how beautiful!

We thus reached the top of a hill. In spite of her high-heeled boots this sprightly young lady of twenty-five darted down the hill like an arrow. I was shamefacedly struggling to get down. She stood at the foot smiling and cheering me and offering to come and drag me. With the greatest difficulty, and crawling at intervals, I somehow managed to scramble to the bottom. She loudly laughed bravo and shamed me all the more as well she might.

Towards the end of my second year in England I came across two Theosophists, brothers, and both unmarried. They talked to me about the *Gita*. They were reading Sir Edwin Arnold s translation *The Song Celestial*—and they invited me to read the original with them. I felt ashamed, as I had read the divine poem neither in Sanskrit nor in Gujarati. **I was constrained to tell them that I had not read the *Gita*,** but that I would gladly read it with them.

I began reading the *Gita* with them. The verses in the second chapter made a deep impression on my mind, and they still ring in my ears. The book struck me as one of priceless worth. The impression has ever since been growing on me with the result that I regard it today as the book *par excellence* for the knowledge of Truth. I have read almost all the

English translations of it, and I regard Sir Edwin Arnold s as the best.

The brothers also recommended *The Light of Asia* by Sir Edwin Arnold, and I read it with even greater interest than I did the *Bhagavadgita*. They also took me on one occasion to the Blavatsky Lodge and introduced me to **Madame Blavatsky** and **Mrs. Besant**. The latter had just then joined the Theosophical Society. The friends advised me to join the Society, but I politely declined saying, 'With my meagre knowledge of my own religion, I do not want to belong to any religious body. I recall having read Madame Blavatsky s *Key to Theosophy*. This book stimulated in me the desire to read books on Hinduism, and disabused me of the notion fostered by the missionaries that Hinduism was rife with superstition.

About the same time I met a good Christian from Manchester in a vegetarian boarding house. He talked to me about Christianity. I narrated to him my Rajkot recollections. He was pained to hear them. He said, I am a vegetarian. I do not drink. Many Christians are meat-eaters and they drink, no doubt; but neither meat-eating nor drinking is enjoined by Scripture. Do please read the Bible. I accepted his advice, and he got me a copy. I began reading it, but I could not possibly read through the Old Testament. I read the book of Genesis, and the chapters that followed invariably sent me to sleep.

But the New Testament produced a different impression, especially the Sermon on the Mount, which went straight to my heart. I compared it with the *Gita*. The verses, But I say unto you, that ye resist not evil: but whosoever shall smite thee on thy right cheek, turn to him the other also. And if any man take away thy coat let him have thy cloak too, delighted me beyond measure. My young mind tried to unify the teaching of the *Gita*, *The Light of Asia* and the Sermon on the Mount.

This reading whetted my appetite for studying the lives of other religious teachers. A friend recommended Carlyle s *Heroes and Hero-Worship.* I read the chapter on the Hero as a prophet and learnt of the Prophet s greatness and bravery and austere living.

And how could I help knowing something of atheism, too? Every Indian knew Bradlaugh s name and his so-called atheism. I read some books about it. It had no effect on me, for I had already crossed the Sahara of atheism. Mrs. Besant, who was then very much in the limelight, had turned to theism from atheism, and that fact also strengthened my aversion to atheism. It was about this time that Bradlaugh died. He was buried in the Woking Cemetery. I attended the funeral, as I believe every Indian residing in London did.

There was a great exhibition at Paris in 1890. I had read about its elaborate preparations, and I also had a keen desire to see Paris. I had heard of a vegetarian restaurant there. I engaged a room and stayed for seven days. I managed everything very economically, both the journey to Paris and the sightseeing there. This I did mostly on foot and with the help of a map of Paris. I have a fair recollection of the Eiffel Tower as I ascended it twice or thrice.

'Called' to the Bar

There were two conditions which had to be fulfilled before a student was formally called to the bar: keeping terms , twelve terms equivalent to about three years; and passing examinations. Keeping terms meant eating one s terms, i.e., attending at least six out of about twenty-four dinners in a term. Eating did not mean actually partaking of the dinner, it meant reporting oneself at the fixed hours and remaining present throughout the dinner. Usually of course everyone ate and drank the good common and choice wines provided. I often ate nothing at these dinners, for the things that I might eat were only bread, boiled potato and cabbage.

Two bottles of wine were allowed to each group of four, and as I did not touch them, I was ever in demand to form a quarter, so that three might empty two bottles. And there was a grand night in each term when extra wines, like champagne, in addition to port and sherry, were served. I was therefore in great demand on that grand night .

I could not see then, nor have I seen since, how these dinners qualified the students better for the bar. **The curriculum of study was easy, barristers being humorously known as dinner-barristers. Everyone knew that the examinations had practically no value.** In my time there were two, one in Roman Law and the other in Common Law. Question papers were easy and examiners were generous. The percentage of passes in the Roman Law examination used to be 95 to 99 and of those in the final examination 75 or even more. And examinations were held not once but four times in a year. But I succeeded in turning them into one. I felt that I should read all the text-books. I decided to read Roman Law in Latin. And all this reading was not without its value later on in South Africa, where Roman-Dutch is the common law. **I passed my examinations, was called to the bar on the 10th of June 1891, and enrolled in the High Court on the 11th.** On the 12th I sailed for home.

But notwithstanding my study there was no end to my helplessness and fear. **I did not feel myself qualified to practise law.** It was easy to be called, but **it was difficult to practise at the bar. I had read the laws, but not learnt how to practise law.** I had read with interest *Legal Maxims*, but did not know how to apply them in my profession. I had read all the leading cases on this maxim, but they gave me no confidence in the application of it in the practice of law.

Besides, **I had learnt nothing at all of Indian law.** I had not the slightest idea of Hindu and Mahomedan law. **I had not even learnt how to draft a plaint,** and felt completely at sea. Pherozeshah Mehta was one who roared like a lion in law courts. How, I wondered, could he have learnt the art in England? **I had serious misgivings as to whether I should be able even to earn a living by the profession.** I confided my difficulties to some of my friends. One of them suggested that I should seek Dadabhai Naoroji s advice. I thought I had no right to trouble such a great man for an interview. Whenever an address by him was announced, I would attend it, listen to him from a corner of the hall, and go away after having feasted my eyes and ears. In course of time, I mustered up courage to present to him the note of introduction. He said: You can come and have my advice whenever you like. But I never availed myself of his offer.

I forget now whether it was the same friend or someone else who recommended me to meet Mr. Frederick Pincott. He was a Conservative, but his affection for Indian students was pure and unselfish. Many students sought his advice and I also applied to him for an appointment, which he granted. He greeted me as a friend. He laughed away my pessimism. Do you think, he said, that everyone must be a Pherozeshah Mehta? Rest assured it takes no unusual skill to be an ordinary lawyer. Common honesty and industry are enough to enable him to make a living. Well, let me know the extent of your general reading.

When I acquainted him with my little stock of reading, he was, as I could see, rather disappointed. He said, I understand your trouble. Your general reading is meagre. **You have no knowledge of the world,** a ***sine qua non*** **for a vakil. You have not even read the history of India. A vakil should know human nature.** I see that you have not even read Kaye and Malleson s history of the mutiny of 1857. Get hold of that at once and also read two more books to understand human nature. These were Lavator s and Shemmelpennick s books on physiognomy.

Thus with just a little leaven of hope mixed with my despair, I landed at Bombay from S.S. Assam.

◆◆◆

Gandhi Flowers

'When your mind is filled
with the light of heaven, all
obstacles in your path
fade away.'

•

3
FAILURE IN INDIA

My elder brother had come to meet me at the dock. I was pining to see my mother. I did not know that she was no more in the flesh to receive me back into her bosom. The sad news was now given me, and I underwent the usual ablution. My brother had kept me ignorant of her death, which took place whilst I was still in England. He wanted to spare me the blow in a foreign land. My grief was even greater than over my father s death.

Friends advised me to go to Bombay for some time in order to gain experience of the High Court, to study Indian law and to try and get what briefs I could. I took up the suggestion and went.

Life in Bombay

In Bombay I started a household with a cook. I began my study of Indian law. My brother, for his part, was trying his best to get me briefs. The study of Indian law was a tedious business. The Civil Procedure Code I could in no way get on with. Not so, however, with the Evidence Act. Virchand Gandhi was reading for the Solicitor s Examination and would tell me all sorts of stories about barristers and vakils.

It is not unusual, he would add, for a barrister to vegetate for five or seven years. You should count yourself lucky if you can paddle your own canoe in three years time. But I had not the courage to conduct a case. I was helpless beyond words, even as the bride come fresh to her father-in-law s house.

My First Case a Failure

About this time, I took up the case of one Mamibai. It was a small cause . You will have to pay some commission to the tout, I was told. I emphatically declined.

It was an easy case. I charged Rs. 30 for my fees. I appeared for the defendant and had thus to cross-examine the plaintiff s witnesses. **I stood up, but my heart sank into my boots. My head was reeling.** I could think of no question to ask. The judge must have laughed, and the vakils no doubt enjoyed the spectacle. But I was past seeing anything. **I sat down and told the agent that I could not conduct the case,** that he would better engage Patel and have the fee from me. Mr. Patel was duly engaged for Rs. 51.

I hastened from the court, not knowing whether my client won or lost her case, but I was ashamed of myself, and decided not to take up any more cases until I had courage enough to conduct them. Indeed **I did not go to court again until I went to South Africa.** There was no virtue in my decision. I had simply made a virtue of necessity.

But there *was* another case in store for me at Bombay. It was a memorial to be drafted. A poor Muslim s land was confiscated in Porbandar. His case appeared to be weak, but I consented to draft a memorial for him. I drafted it and read it out to friends. They approved of it, and that to some extent made me feel confident that I was qualified enough to draft a memorial.

For a Teacher's Job

I thought I might take up a teacher s job. My knowledge of English was good enough, and I should have loved to teach English to Matriculation boys in some school. I came across an advertisement in the papers: Wanted, an English teacher to teach one hour daily. Salary Rs. 75. I applied for the post and was called for an interview. I went there in high spirits, but **when the principal found that I was not a graduate, he regretfully refused me.**

But I have passed the London Matriculation with Latin as my second language.

'True, but we want a graduate.'

I wrung my hands in despair. My brother also felt much worried. We both came to the conclusion that it was no use spending more time in Bombay. I should settle in Rajkot where my brother, himself a petty pleader, could give me some work. I used to attend High Court daily whilst in Bombay, but I cannot say that I learnt anything there. I had not sufficient knowledge to learn much. Often I could not follow the cases and dozed off.

I left Bombay and went to Rajkot where I set up my own office. **Here I got along moderately well.**

Drafting applications and memorials brought me in, on an average, Rs. 300 a month. Here I had to compromise the principle of giving no commission, which in Bombay I had so scrupulously observed. Whilst in Bombay commissions had to be paid to touts, here they had to be paid to vakils who briefed you.

Opportunity in Africa

In the meantime a Meman firm from Porbandar wrote to my brother making the following offer: We have business in South Africa. Ours is a big firm, and we have a big case there in the Court, our claim being £ 40,000. We have engaged the services of the best vakils and barristers. If you sent your brother there, he would be useful to us and also to himself. He would be able to instruct our counsel better than ourselves.

My brother introduced me to Sheth Abdul Karim Jhaveri, a partner of Dada Abdulla and Co., the firm in question. It won t be a difficult job, the Sheth assured me. We have big Europeans as our friends. You can be useful to us in our shop. Much of our correspondence is in English and you can help us with that too.

How long do you require my services? I asked. And what will be the payment?

Not more than a year. We will pay you a first class return fare and a sum of £ 105, all found.

This was hardly going there as a barrister. It was going as a servant of the firm. But I wanted somehow to leave India.

◆◆◆

4

THREE YEARS IN S. AFRICA

Age 23-26

As the ship arrived at the quay, I observed that the Indians were not held in much respect. I could not fail to notice a sort of snobbishness about the manner in which those who knew Abdulla Sheth behaved towards him, and it stung me. Those who looked at me did so with a certain amount of curiosity. My dress marked me out from other Indians. I had a frock-coat and a turban.

I was taken to the firm s quarters and shown into the room set apart for me, next to Abdulla Sheth s. He did not understand me. He thought his brother had sent him a white elephant. My style of dress and living struck him as being expensive like that of the Europeans.

There was no particular work then which could be given me. Their case was going on in the Transvaal. There was no meaning in sending me there immediately. And how far could he trust my ability and honesty? He would not be in Pretoria to watch me. The defendants were in Pretoria, and they might bring undue influence to bear on me. And if work in connection with the case in question was not to be entrusted to me, what work would I be given to do, as all other work could be done much better by his clerks?

Abdulla Sheth was practically unlettered, but he had a rich fund of experience. By practice he had picked up just sufficient English for conversational purposes. The Indians held him in very high esteem. His firm was then the biggest, or at any rate one of the biggest, of the Indian firms. With all these advantages he had one disadvantage he was by nature suspicious. He was proud of Islam and loved to discourse on Islamic philosophy.

Take Off your Turban

On the second or third day of my arrival, he took me to see the Durban court. There he introduced me to several people and seated me next to his attorney. The Magistrate kept staring at me and finally asked me to take off my turban. This I refused to do and left the court.

I could see that the Indians were divided into different groups. One was that of Muslim merchants, who would call themselves Arabs . Another was that of Hindu, and yet another of Parsi clerks. The Hindu clerks were neither here nor there, unless they cast in their lot with the 'Arabs . The Parsi clerks would call themselves Persians. These three classes had some social relations with one another. But by far the classes was that composed of Tamil, Telugu and North Indian indentured and freed labourers. Englishmen called them coolies , and as the majority of Indians belonged to the labouring class, all Indians were called 'coolies , or *'samis'*. *'Sami'* is a Tamil suffix occurring after many Tamil names.

I was hence known as a coolie barrister . The merchants were known as coolie merchants . The Muslim merchant would resent this and say: I am not a coolie, I am an Arab, or I am a merchant, and the Englishman, if courteous, would apologize to him. The question of wearing the turban had a great importance in this state of things. Being obliged to take off one s Indian turban would be pocketing an insult. **So I thought I had better bid good-bye to the Indian turban and begin wearing an English hat**.

But Abdulla Sheth disapproved of the idea. He said, If you do anything of the kind, it will have a very bad effect. You will compromise those insisting on wearing Indian turbans. And an Indian turban sits well on your head. If you wear an English hat, you will pass for a waiter.

I liked Abdulla Sheth s advice. I wrote to the press about the incident and defended the wearing of my turban in the court. The question was very much discussed in the papers, which described me as an unwelcome visitor . Thus **the incident gave me an unexpected advertisement in South Africa within a few days of my arrival there.**

The firm received a letter from their lawyer saying that preparations should be made for the case, and that Abdulla Sheth should go to Pretoria himself or send a representative. As I began to study the case, I felt as though I ought to begin from the ABC of the subject. It was all Greek to me. Book-keeping I had learnt neither at school nor during my stay in England. And the case for which I had come to South Africa was mainly about accounts. I purchased a book on book-keeping and studied it. That gave me some confidence. I understood the case. I was prepared to go to Pretoria.

Where will you put up? asked the Sheth.

Wherever you want me to, said I.

Then I shall write to our lawyer. He will arrange for your lodgings. I shall also write to my Meman friends there, but I would not advise you to stay with them. The other party has great influence in Pretoria. Should anyone of them manage to read our private correspondence, it might do us much harm. The more you avoid familiarity with them, the better for us.

Don t worry. Not a soul shall know anything that is confident between us. But I do intend cultivating the acquaintance of the other party. I should like to be friends with them. I would try, if possible, to settle the case out of court. After all Tyeb Sheth is a relative of yours.

The mention of a probable settlement somewhat startled the Sheth.

Y....es, I see. There would be nothing better than a settlement out of court. But we are all relatives and know one another very well indeed. Tyeb Sheth is not a man to consent to a settlement easily. With the slightest unwariness on our part, he would screw all sorts of things out of us, and do us down in the end. So please think twice before you do anything.

'Don t be anxious about that, said I. I need not talk to Tyeb Sheth about the case. I would only suggest to him to come to an understanding, and so save a lot of necessary litigation.'

Insults that made him Gandhi

On the seventh or eighth day after my arrival, I left Durban. A first class seat was booked for me.

The train reached Maritzburg, the capital of Natal, at about 9 p.m. Beddings used to be provided at this station. A railway servant came and asked me if I wanted one. No, said I, I have one with me. A passenger came next, and looked me up and down. He saw that I was a coloured man. This disturbed him. Out he went and came in again with one or two officials. They all kept quiet, when another official came to me and said, Come along, you must go to the van compartment.

But I have a first class ticket, said I.

That doesn t matter, rejoined the other.

I tell you, I was permitted to travel in this compartment at Durban, and I insist on going on in it.

No, you won t, said the official. You must leave this compartment, or else I shall have to call a police constable to push you out.

Yes, you may. I refuse to get out voluntarily.

The constable came. He took me by the hand

Gandhi arrived in India
in this dress, with Kasturba

'One who has appreciated
the value of studies
is a student all his life.'

'Animated by a gay teasing ... This is how the Mahatma teased the Viceroy in his own palace...when handed a cup of tea, he poured a bit of salt into it out of a paper hidden in his shawl and remarked smilingly, "to remined us of the famous Boston Tea Party."'

—***Erik. H. Erikson***

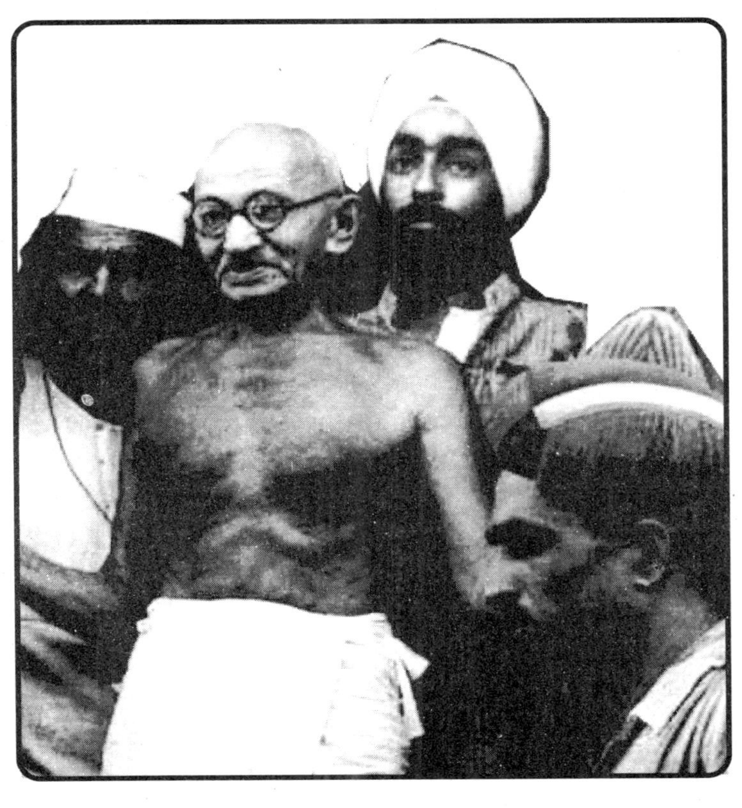

Gandhi travelled in the IIIrd Class always.

'I am uncompromising in the matter
of women's right;
She should labour under no legal
disability not suffered by men.
I should treat the
daughters and sons on a
footing of perfect equality.'

A Tid-bit

At Noakhali, where he went
to restore peace, he started
his day at 2.30 by learning Bengali by
poring over his Bengali primer.

With a Buddhist monk

'A coward is incapable
of exhibiting love;
it is the prerogative
of the brave.'

'It is true that Gandhi "compromised" with the rich—those untouchables of the class struggle—but he also "compromised" with the poor, spending at least as much time in the untouchables' quarters. He seems to have regarded the capitalist as well as the garbage-man as his social equal.'

—*Dwight Macdonald*

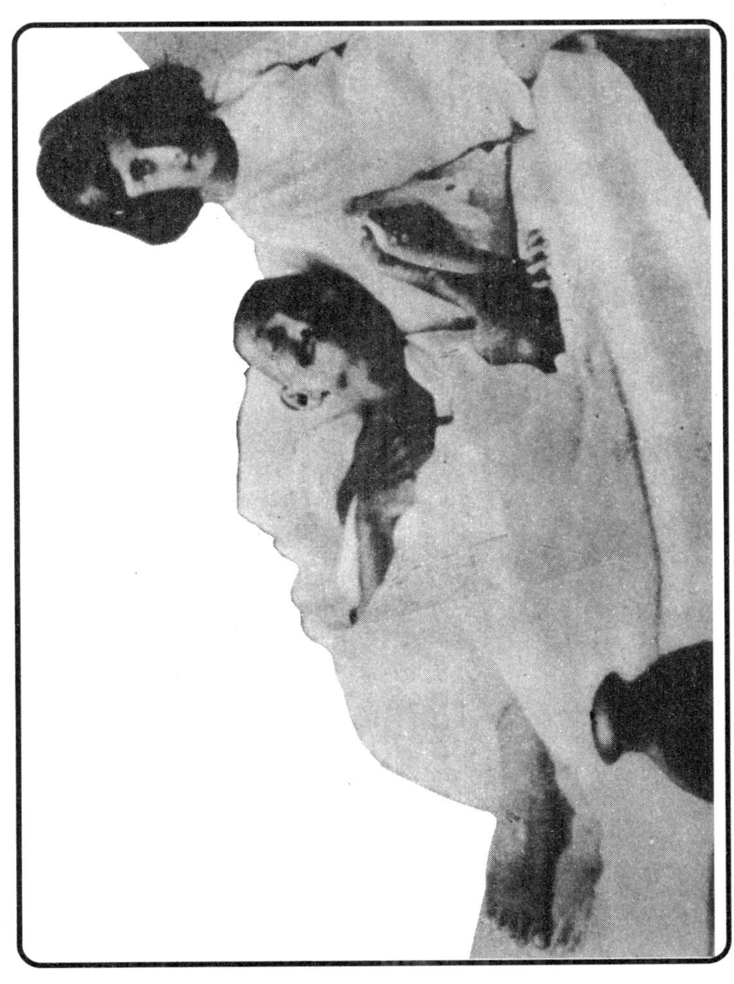

With Indira as a girl— on his sickbed

'Untouchability
as it is practised in Hinduism today
is in my opinion
a sin against God and man
and is like a
poison slowly eating into the very
vitals of Hinduism.
In my opinion
it has no sanction whatsoever
in the Hindu Shastras.'

'So this was Gandhi...I watched
his face...and tried to think
what little animal he reminds
me of...could this be the man
who had shaken the British Raj
to its foundations?'

—Paul Roche

and pushed me out. My luggage was also taken out. I refused to go to the other compartment and the train steamed away. I went and sat in the waiting room, keeping my handbag with me, and leaving the other luggage where it was. The railway authorities had taken charge of it.

It was winter, and the cold was extremely bitter. My overcoat was in my luggage, but I did not dare to ask for it lest I should be insulted again, so I sat and shivered. **I began to think of my duty. Should I fight for my rights or go back to India, or should I go on to Pretoria without minding the insults,** and return to India after finishing the case? The hardship to which I was subjected was superficial only a symptom of the deep disease of colour prejudice. **I should try, if possible, to root out the disease and suffer hardships in the process.**

So I decided to take the next available train to Pretoria. The following morning I sent a long telegram to the General Manager of the Railway and also informed Abdulla Sheth, who immediately met the General Manager. The Manager justified the conduct of the railway authorities, but informed him that he had already instructed the Station Master to see that I reached my destination safely. Abdulla Sheth wired to the Indian merchants in Maritzburg and to friends in other places to meet me and look after me. The merchants came to see me at the station and tried to comfort me by narrating their own hardships and explaining that what had happened to me was nothing unusual.

The evening train arrived. There was a reserved berth for me.

The train took me to Charlestown. There was no railway, in those days between Charlestown and Johannesburg, but only a stage-coach. I possessed a ticket for the coach. Abdulla Sheth had sent a wire to the coach agent at Charlestown.

Physical Assault

But the agent only needed a pretext for putting me off, and so, he said, Your ticket is cancelled. The reason at the back of his mind was not want of accommodation, but quite another. Passengers had to be accommodated inside the coach, but as I was regarded as a coolie and looked a stranger, it would be proper, thought the leader , as the white man in charge of the coach was called, not to seat me with the white passengers. There were seats on either side of the coachbox. The leader sat on one of these as a rule. Today he sat inside and gave me his seat.

At about three o clock the coach reached Pardekoph. Now the leader desired to sit where I was seated, as he wanted to smoke. So he took a piece of dirty sackcloth from the driver, spread it on the footboard and, addressing me, said, Sami, you sit on this, I want to sit near the driver. In fear and trembling I said to him, It was you who seated me here, though I should have been accommodated inside.

As I was struggling through these sentences, **the man came down upon me and began to heavily box my ears. He seized me by the arm and tried**

to drag me down. I clung to the brass rails of the coachbox and was determined to keep my hold even at the risk of breaking my wristbones. He was strong and I was weak. Some of the passengers were moved to pity and exclaimed: Man, let him alone. Don t beat him. He is not to blame. He is right. If he can t stay there, let him come and sit with us. No fear, cried the man, but he seemed somewhat crestfallen and stopped beating me.

The passengers took their seats and, the whistle given, the coach rattled away. The man cast an angry look at me now and then and, pointing his finger at me, growled: Take care, let me once get to Standerton and I shall show you what I do.

After dark we reached Standerton and I heaved a sigh of relief on seeing some Indian faces. As soon as I got down, these friends said: We are here to receive you and take you to Isa Sheth s shop. We have had a telegram from Dada Abdulla. I was very glad, and we went to Sheth Isa Haji Sumar s shop.

Abdulla Sheth had wired to Johannesburg and their man had come to receive me, but neither did I see him nor did he recognize me. So I decided to go to a hotel. Taking a cab I asked to be driven to the Grand National Hotel. I saw the Manager and asked for a room. He eyed me for a moment, and politely saying, I am very sorry, we are full up,' bade me good-bye. So I asked the cabman to drive to Muhammad Kasam Kamruddin s shop. Here I found Abdul Gani Sheth expecting me, and he had a hearty laugh over the story of my experience at the hotel.

However did you expect to be admitted to a hotel? he said.

Why not?

You will come to know after you have stayed here a few days, said he. Only *we* can live in a land like this, because, for making money, we do not mind pocketing insults...

Look now, you have to go to Pretoria tomorrow. You will *have* to travel third class. Conditions in the Transvaal are worse than in Natal. First and second class tickets are never issued to Indians.

I said to the Sheth: I wish to go first class, and if I cannot, I shall prefer to take a cab to Pretoria.

Ticket on a Condition

Sheth Abdul Gani agreed to my proposal to travel first, and accordingly we sent a note to the Station Master. I mentioned in my note that I was a barrister and that I always travelled first. I also stated in the letter that I needed to reach Pretoria as early as possible, that as there was no time to await his reply I would receive it in person at the station. I went to the station in a frock-coat and necktie, placed a sovereign for my fare on the counter and asked for a first class ticket.

You sent me that note? he asked.

That is so. I shall be much obliged if you will give me a ticket.

He smiled and, moved to pity, said: I am not a Transvaaler. I am a Hollander. I appreciate your feelings, and you have my sympathy. I do want to give you a ticket on one condition, however, that, **if the guard should ask you to shift to the third class, you will not involve me in the affair, by which I mean that you should proceed against the Railway Company.** I wish you a safe journey.

With these words he booked the ticket. I thanked him and gave him the necessary assurance.

I took my seat in a first class compartment and the train started. At Germiston the guard came to examine the tickets. He was angry to find me there, and signalled to me with his finger to go to the third class. I showed him my first class ticket. That doesn t matter, said he, move to the third class.

There was only one English passenger in the compartment. He took the guard to task. What do you mean by troubling the gentleman? I do not mind in the least his travelling with me.

The guard muttered: If you want to travel with a coolie, do I care? and went away.

At about 8 o clock in the evening the train reached Pretoria. I wondered where to go, as I feared that no hotel would accept me.

The station became clear of all passengers. I gave my ticket to the ticket collector and began my inquiries. An American Negro who was standing nearby broke into the conversation.

I see, said he, that you are an utter stranger here, without any friends. If you will come with me, I will take you to a small hotel, of which the proprietor is an American, who is very well known to me. I think he will accept you.

He took me to Johnston s Family Hotel. He drew Mr. Johnston aside to speak to him, and the latter agreed to accommodate me for the night, on condition that I should have my dinner served in my room. I assure you, said he, that I have no colour prejudice. But I have only European customers, and, if I allowed you to eat in the dining-room, my guests might be offended and even go away.

I was shown into a room, where I now sat waiting for the dinner and musing, as I had expected the waiter to come very shortly with the dinner. Instead Mr. Johnston appeared. He said: I was ashamed of having asked you to have your dinner here. So I spoke to the other guests about you, and asked them if they would mind your having your dinner in the dining-room. They said they had no objection. Please, therefore, come to the dining-room, if you will, and stay here as long as you wish.

I thanked him again, went to the dining-room and had a hearty dinner.

Stay with a Poor Baker

Next morning I called on the attorney, Mr. A. W. Baker. He received me very warmly and made kind inquiries. He said: We have no work for you here as barrister, for we have engaged the best counsel. So I shall take your assistance only to the extent of getting necessary information. I have not yet found rooms for you. There is a fearful amount of colour prejudice here, and therefore it is not easy to find lodgings for such as you. But I know a poor woman.

She is the wife of a baker. I think she will take you. Come, let us go to her place.

So he took me to her house. He spoke with her privately about me, and she agreed to accept me as a boarder at 35 shillings a week.

Mr. Baker, besides being an attorney, was a staunch lay preacher. During the very first interview he ascertained my religious views. I said to him: I am a Hindu by birth. And yet I do not know much of Hinduism, and I know less of other religions. In fact I do not know where I am, and what is and what should be my belief. I intend to make a careful study of my own religion and, as far as I can, of other religions as well.

Mr. Baker was glad to hear all this, and said: I am one of the Directors of the South Africa General Mission. I have built a church at my own expense, and deliver sermons in it regularly. I am free from colour prejudice. I have some co-workers, and we meet at one o clock every day for a few minutes and pray for peace and light. I shall be glad if you will join us there. I shall give you, besides, some religious books to read, though of course the book of books is the Holy Bible.

The next day at one o clock I went to Mr. Baker s prayer-meeting. There I was introduced to Miss Harris, Miss Gabb, Mr. Coates and others. Everyone kneeled down to pray, and I followed suit. A prayer was now added for my welfare: Lord, show the path to the new brother who has come amongst us. Give him, Lord, the peace that Thou hast given us. May the Lord Jesus who has saved us save him too.

The Misses Harris and Gabb were both elderly maiden ladies. Mr. Coates was a Quaker. The two ladies lived together, and they gave me a standing invitation to four o clock tea at their house every Sunday.

When we met on Sunday, I used to give Mr. Coates my religious diary for the week, and discuss with him the books I had read and the impression they had left on me. The ladies used to narrate their sweet experiences and talk about the peace they had found. Mr. Coates was a frank-hearted staunch young man. He began to give me books of his own choice, until my shelf was filled with them.

I read a number of such books in 1893. Parts of these were unintelligible to me. I liked some things in them, while I did not like others. *Many Infallible Proofs* were proofs in support of the religion of the Bible. The book had no effect on me. Parker s *Commentary* was morally stimulating but it could not be of any help to one who had no faith in the prevalent Christian beliefs.

But Mr. Coates was not the man easily to accept defeat. He saw, round my neck, the Vaishnava necklace of Tulsi-beads. He thought it to be superstition, and was pained by it. This superstition does not become you. Come, let me break the necklace.

No, you will not. It is a sacred gift from my mother.

But do you believe in it?

I do not know its mysterious significance. I do

not think I should come to harm if I did not wear it. But I cannot, without sufficient reason, give up a necklace that she put round my neck out of love and in the conviction that it would be conducive to my welfare.

Launching a Movement

Sheth Tyeb Haji Khan Muḥammad had in Pretoria the same position as was enjoyed by Dada Abdulla in Natal. I made his acquaintance the very first week and told him of my intention to get in touch with every Indian in Pretoria. I expressed a desire to study the conditions of Indians there, and asked for his help in my work, which he gladly agreed to give.

My first step was to call a meeting of all the Indians in Pretoria and to present to them a picture of their condition in the Transvaal. It was principally attended by Meman merchants.

My speech at this meeting may be said to have been the first public speech in my life. I went fairly prepared with my **subject, which was about observing truthfulness in business.** I had always heard the merchants say that truth was not possible in business. Business, they say, is a very practical affair, and truth a matter of religion. Pure truth, they hold, is out of the question in business, one can speak it only so far as is suitable. **I strongly contested the position in my speech and awakened the merchants to a sense of their duty, which was twofold. Their responsibility to be truthful was all the greater in a foreign**

land, because the conduct of a few Indians was the measure of that of the millions of their fellow-countrymen.

I had found our people s habits to be insanitary, as compared with those of the Englishmen around them, and drew their attention to it. I laid stress on the necessity of forgetting all distinctions such as Hindus, Muslims, Parsis, Christians, Gujaratis, Madrasis, Punjabis, Sindhis, Kachchhis, Surtis and so on. **I suggested, in conclusion, the formation of an association to make representations to the authorities** concerned and offered to place at its disposal as much of my time and service as was possible.

I saw that I made a considerable impression on the meeting. My speech was followed by discussion. I felt encouraged. I saw that very few amongst my audience knew English. As I felt that knowledge of English would be useful in that country, **I advised those who had leisure to learn English.** I undertook to teach a class, if one was started, or personally to instruct individuals desiring to learn the language.

The class was not started, but three young men expressed their readiness to learn at their convenience, and on condition that I went to their places to teach them. Of these, two were Muslims one of them a barber and the other a clerk and the third was a Hindu, a petty shopkeeper. Sometimes it happened that I would go to their places only to find them engaged in their business. None of the three desired a deep study of English, but two may

Gandhi (L) with his secretary Sonia Schlesin and close friend Kallenbach, at Phoenix. They learnt shoe-making, carpentary, etc., to run the self-sufficient settlement.

'All religions proceed from
the same God
but all are imperfect
because they have come
down to us
through imperfect human
instrumentality.'

'When the century closes, Gandhi and his followers—whether in Asia, Africa or America—may go down as the influencial men of our time...because they were imaginative artists who knew how to use world politics as their stage.'

—*Ved Mehta*

With G.K. Gokhale—
his great support in India

'If we do not account for
every single pie we receive
and do not make
judicious use of the funds ,
we shall deserve to be
blotted out of public life.
Public money belongs to the
poor public of India.'

'Gandhi belongs to tomorrow.'

—*Ralph Templin*

With G.K. Gokhale—
his great support in India

'If we do not account for
every single pie we receive
and do not make
judicious use of the funds ,
we shall deserve to be
blotted out of public life.
Public money belongs to the
poor public of India.'

'Gandhi belongs to tomorrow.'

—***Ralph Templin***

*With Mohammad Ali Jinnah—
who made Pakistan*

'I am convinced that the masses
do not want to fight
if
the leaders do not.'

A Tid-bit

Gandhi said to Amrit Kaur on Jan. 28, 1948: 'If I am to die by the bullet of a mad man, I must do so smiling. You promise me that you are not to shed one tear.'

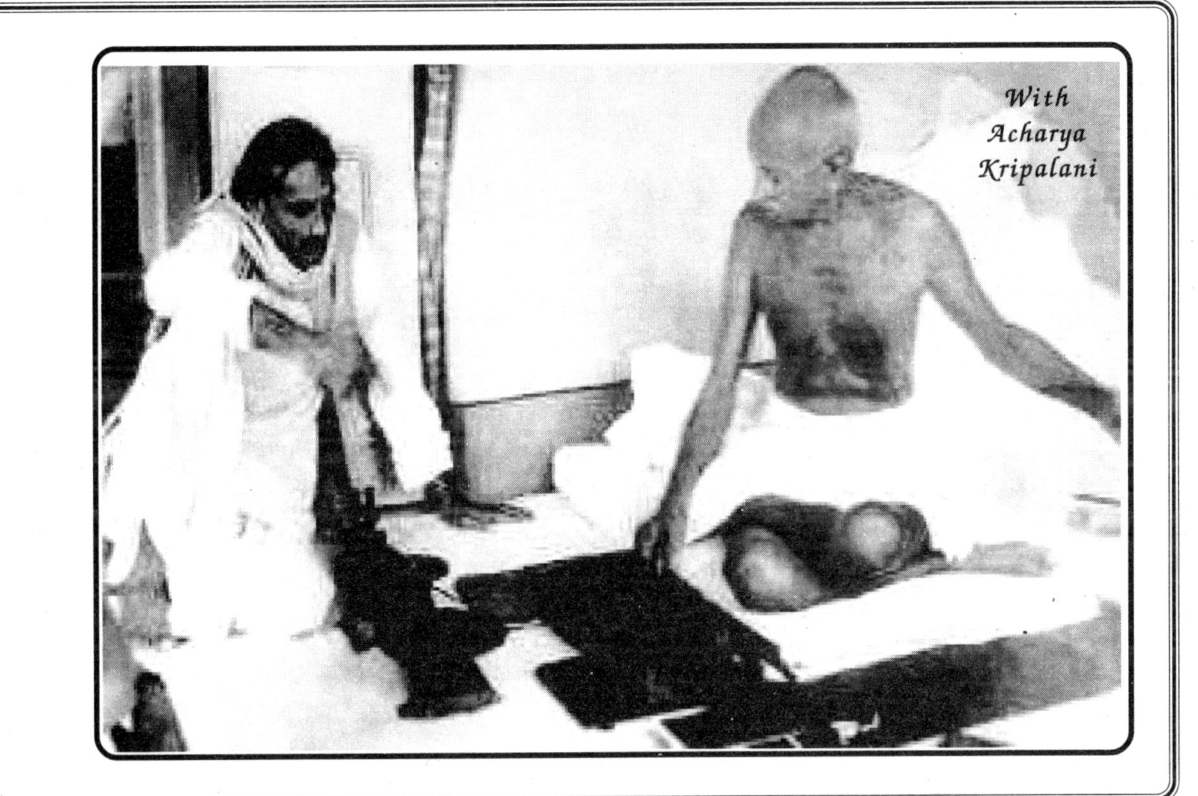

With Acharya Kripalani

'I have known the
serious consequences
overtaking
organizations that have counted
private character as
a matter of no consequence.'

'Gandhi has done his part. It
now remains for the people of
India to take upon themselves his
world leadership for non-violence...
Oh!, India, dare to be worthy of your
Gandhi!'

—***Pearl Buck***

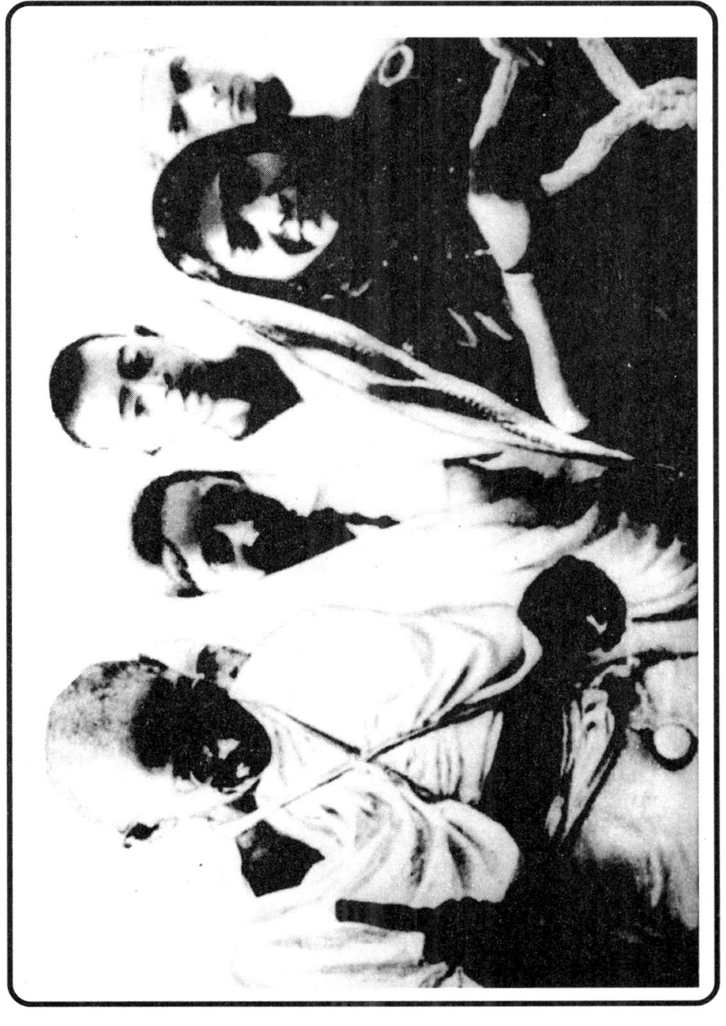

With Sarojini Naidu

'Action for one's own self binds,
Action for the sake of others
delivers from bondage.'

'The horror of Gandhi murder
lies in the fact tht any man
could look into the face of this
extraordinary person and
deliberately pull a trigger.'

—Mary McCarthy

be said to have made fairly good progress in about eight months. Two learnt enough to keep accounts and write ordinary business letters.

It was decided to hold such meetings, and on these occasions there was a free exchange of ideas. **The result was that there was now in Pretoria no Indian I did not know. This prompted me in turn to make the acquaintance of the British Agent in Pretoria,** Mr. Jacobus de Web. **He agreed to help us as best he could and invited me to meet him whenever I wished.**

I now communicated with the railway authorities. **I got a letter in reply to the effect that first and second class tickets would be issued to Indians who were properly dressed.** It rested with the Station Master to decide who was 'properly dressed.'

In short, my stay in Pretoria enabled me to make a deep study of the social, economic and political condition of the Indians in the Transvaal and the Orange Free State. I had no idea that this study was to be of invaluable service to me in the future. For I had thought of returning home by the end of the year. But God disposed otherwise.

In the Orange Free State the Indians were deprived of all their rights by a special law enacted in 1888 or even earlier. If they chose to stay there, they could do so only to serve as waiters in hotels or to pursue some other such menial calling. The traders were driven away with a nominal compensation. They made representations and petitions, but in vain.

A very stringent enactment was passed in the Transvaal that all Indians should pay a poll tax of £ 3 as fee for entry into the Transvaal. They might not own land except in locations set apart for them, and in practice even that was not to be ownership. They had no franchise. The laws for the coloured people were also applied. Under these latter, **Indians might not walk on pubic footpaths and might not move out of doors after 9 p.m. without a permit.** The enforcement of this last regulation was elastic so far as the Indians were concerned. Those who passed as Arabs were, as a matter of favour, exempted from it. The exemption depended on the sweet will of the police.

The consequences of the regulation regarding the use of footpaths were rather serious for me. I always went out for a walk through President Street to an open plain. Now the man on duty used to be changed from time to time. Once one of these men, **without giving me the slighest warning, without even asking me to leave the footpath, pushed and kicked me into the street.**

I never again went through this street.

The incident deepened my feeling for the Indian settlers. I discussed with them the advisability of making a test case, if it were found necessary to do so, after having seen the British Agent in the matter of these regulations.

Setting the Case

Dada Abdulla s was no small case. The suit was for £ 40,000. Arising out of business transactions, it was full of intricacies of accounts. I approached Tyeb Sheth and requested and advised him to go to arbitration. I suggested to him that, if an arbitrator commanding the confidence of both parties could be appointed, the case would be quickly finished. The lawyers fees were so rapidly mounting up that they were enough to devour all the resources of the clients. The case occupied so much of their attention that they had no time left for any other work. **I strained every nerve to bring about a compromise. At last Tyeb Sheth agreed. An arbitrator was appointed, the case was argued before him, and Dada Abdulla won.**

But that did not satisfy me. If my client were to seek immediate execution of the award, it would be impossible for Tyeb Sheth to meet. It was impossible for Tyeb Sheth to pay down the whole sum of about £37,000 and costs. There was only one way. Dada Abdulla should allow him to pay in moderate instalments. He was equal to the occasion, and granted Tyeb Sheth instalments spread over a very long period. **Both were happy over the result, and both rose in public estimation. My joy was boundless. I had learnt the true practice of law. I had learnt to find out the better side of human nature and to enter men s hearts.** The lesson was so indelibly burnt into me that large part of my time during the twenty years of my practice as a lawyer was occupied in **bringing about private compromises of hundreds of cases.**

Efforts to Convert

As Christian friends were endeavouring to convert me, even so were Muslim friends. Abdulla Sheth had kept on inducing me to study Islam, and of course he had always something to say regarding its beauty.

I purchased Sale s translation of the Koran and began reading it. I also obtained other books on Islam. I communicated with Christian friends in England. One of them introduced me to Edward Maitland, with whom I opened correspondence. He sent me *The Perfect Way,* a book he had written in collaboration with Anna Kingsford. The book was a repudiation of the current Christian belief. He also sent me another book, *The New Interpretation of the Bible.* I liked both. **They seemed to support Hinduism. Tolstoy s *The Kingdom of God is Within You* overwhelmed me.** It left an abiding impression on me. Though I took a path my Christian friends had not intended for me, I have remained for ever indebted to them for the religious quest that they awakened in me.

The case having been concluded, I had no reason for staying in Pretoria. So I went back to Durban and began to make preparations for my return home. But Abdulla Sheth was not the man to let me sail without a send-off. He gave a farewell party in my honour at Sydenham.

A New Step

Whilst I was turning over the sheets of some of the newspapers I found there, I chanced to see a paragraph in a corner of one of them under the caption Indian Franchise . It was with reference to the Bill then before the House of Legislature, which sought to deprive the Indians of their right to elect members of the Natal Legislative Assembly. I was ignorant of the Bill, and so were the rest of the guests who had assembled there.

I inquired of Abdulla Sheth about it. He said: What can we understand in these matters? As you know all our trade in the Orange Free State has been swept away. We agitated about it, but in vain. We are after all lame men, being unlettered. What can we know of legislation? Our eyes and ears are the European attorneys here.

But, said I, there are so many young Indians born and educated here. Do not they help you?

They! exclaimed Abdulla Sheth in despair, they never care to come to us. Being Christians, they are under the thumb of the white clergymen, who in their turn are subject to the Government.

The other guests were listening to this conversation with attention. One of them said: Shall I tell you what should be done? **You cancel your passage by this boat, stay here a month longer, and we will fight as you direct us.**

All the others chimed in: Indeed! indeed! Abdulla Sheth, you must detain Gandhibhai.

The Sheth was a shrewd man. He said: You have as much right as I to do so. Let us *all* persuade him to stay on. But you should remember that he is a barrister. What about his fees?

The mention of fees pained me, and I broke in: Abdulla Sheth, fees are out of the question. There can be no fees for public work. I am prepared to stay a month longer. There is one thing, however. Though you need not pay me anything, work of the nature we contemplate cannot be done without some funds to start with.

And a chorus of voices was heard: Allah is great and merciful. Money will come in. Men there are, as many as you may need. You please consent to stay, and all will be well.

The farewell party was thus turned into a working committee. I worked out in my own mind an outline of the campaign. Thus God laid the foundations of my life in South Africa and sowed the seed of the fight for national self-respect.

Fight Starts

Sheth Haji Muhammad Haji Dada was regarded as the foremost leader of the Indian community in Natal in 1893. A meeting was held under his presidentship at the house of Abdulla Sheth, at which **it was resolved to offer opposition to the Franchise Bill.** Volunteers were enrolled. Natal-born Indians, mostly Christian Indian youths, had been invited to attend this meeting.

Many of the local merchants were of course enrolled, To be invited thus to take part was a new experience in their lives.

The Bill had already been passed, or was about to pass its second reading. In the speeches on the

With Chakravarti Rajagopalachari, who became the first Governor General of Free India

'What
is faith worth
if
it is not translated
into
action.'

'...When I think of Gandhi, I think of Jesus Christ. He lives his life. he speaks his word; he suffers, strives and will some day nobly die for his kingdom upon earth.'

—John Haynes Homes

With Netaji Subhash

'Ahimsa is the highest ideal.
It is meant for the brave
never for the cowardly.'

'All religions belonged to
Gandhi. He had said, "I consider
myself a Hindu, Christian, Muslim,
Jain, Buddhist and Confuian."'

—*Welthy Fisher*

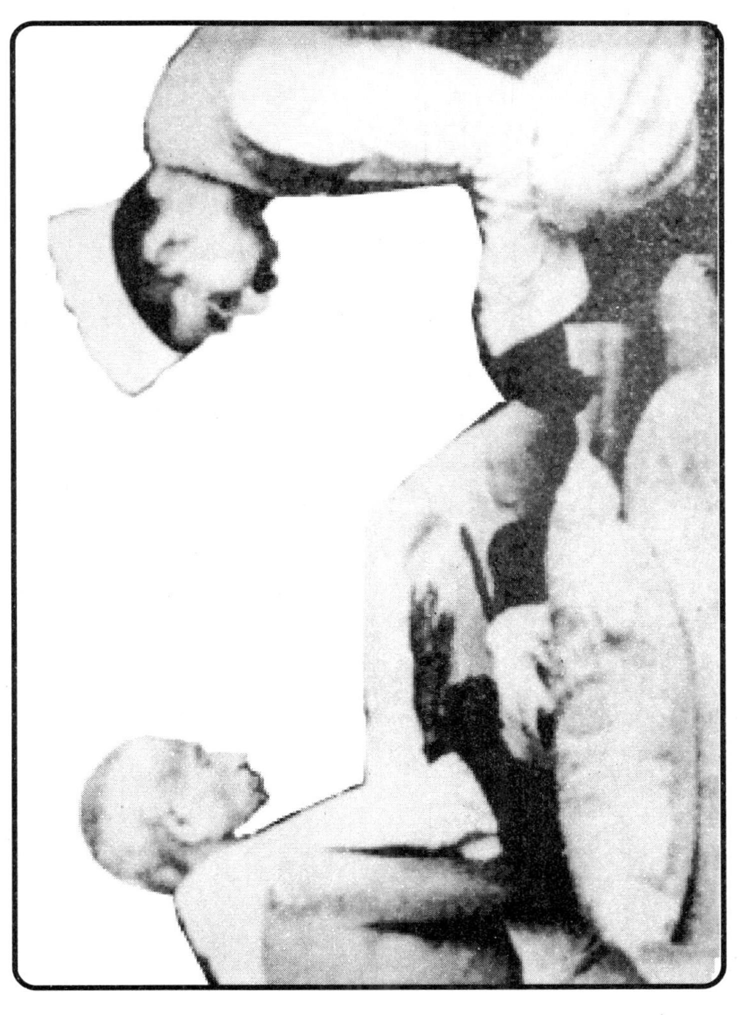

With Dr. Rajendra Prasad,
who became the first President of India.

'The greater the institution, the
greater the chances of abuse.
Democracy is a great insititution
and therefore
liable to be greatly abused.
The remedy is
not
avoidance of democracy
but
reduction of possibility of abuse
to a minimum.'

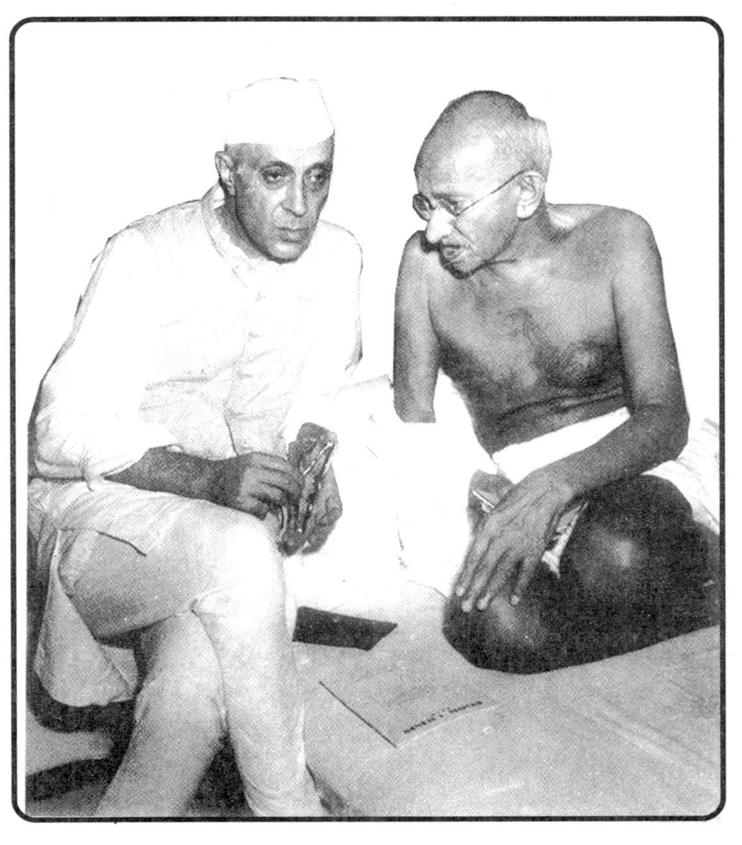

With Jawahar Lal Nehru

'One man cannot do right
in one department of life
whilst
he is occupied in doing wrong
in any other department.
Life is an indivisible whole.'

'...I salute Gandhi's life and
feel the sharp impact of the
spirit which through him
was released into the modern
world.'

—Howard Thurman

occasion **the fact that Indians had expressed no opposition to the stringent Bill was urged as proof of their unfitness for the franchise.**

The first thing we did was to despatch a telegram to the Speaker of the Assembly requesting him to postpone further discussion on the Bill. A similar telegram was sent to the Premier, Sir John Robinson, and another to Mr. Escombe as a friend of Dada Abdulla s. The speaker promptly replied that discussion of the Bill would be postponed for two days. This gladdened our hearts.

The petition to be presented to the Legislative Assembly was drawn up. Three copies had to be prepared and one extra was needed for the press. It was also proposed to obtain as many signatures to it as possible, and **all this work had to be done in the course of a night.** This was accomplished in quick time and the petition was despatched. The newspapers published it with favourable comments. **It likewise created an impression on the Assembly.** It was discussed in the House. Partisans of the Bill offered a defence. The Bill, however, was passed.

Lord Ripon was at this time Secretary of State for the Colonies. It was decided to submit to him a monster petition. Volunteers were enlisted, and all did their due share of the work. Ten thousand signatures were obtained in the course of a fortnight. The villages were scattered at long distances. Dada Abdulla s house became at once a caravanserai and a public office.

The petition was at last submitted. A thousand copies had been printed for circulation and distribution. **It acquainted the Indian public for the first time with conditions in Natal.** Copies were sent to journals and publicists in England representing different parties. The London *Times* supported our claims, and we began to entertain hopes of the Bill being vetoed.

It was now impossible for me to leave Natal. The Indian friends surrounded me on all sides and importuned me to remain there permanently. I expressed my difficulties. I had made up my mind not to stay at public expense. I therefore decided that I could stay only if the members of the community guaranteed legal work to support me.

About twenty merchants gave me retainer for one year for their legal work. Besides this, Dada Abdulla purchased me the necessary furniture in lieu of a purse he had intended to give me on my departure. Thus I settled in Natal.

I applied for admission as an advocate of the Supreme Court. The Law Society sprang a surprise on me by serving me with a notice opposing my application for admission. But the main objection was that, when the regulations regarding admission of advocates were made, the possibility of a coloured man applying could not have been contemplated.

The Supreme Court ruled out the opposition without even calling upon Mr. Escombe to reply. The Chief Justice said in effect: Court has no authority to prevent Mr. Gandhi from being enrolled as an advocate. We admit his application. Mr. Gandhi, you can take the oath.'

The opposition of the Law Society gave me another advertisement in South Africa. Most of the newspapers condemned the opposition and accused the Law Society of jealousy.

Natal Indian Congress Started

Sustained agitation was essential for making an impression on the Secretary of State for the Colonies. For this purpose it was thought necessary to bring into being a permanent organization. I recommended that the organization should be called the Natal Indian Congress, and on the 22nd May the Natal Indian Congress came into being.

Meetings used to be held once a month or even once a week if required. Minutes of the proceedings would be read, and all sorts of questions would be discussed. Another feature of the Congress was service of Colonial-born educated Indians. **The Colonial-born Indian Educational Association was founded under the auspices of the Congress.**

The third feature of the Congress was propaganda. With that end in view I wrote two pamphlets. The first was *An Appeal to Every Briton in South Africa.* It contained a statement, supported by evidence, of the general condition of Natal Indians. The other was entitled *The Indian Franchise—An Appeal.*

Although the members of the Natal Indian Congress included the Colonial-born Indians and the clerical class, the unskilled wage-earners, the indentured labourers were still outside its pale. They could not afford to belong to it by paying the subscription. The Congress could win their attachment only by serving them. An opportunity offered itself when neither the Congress nor I was really ready for it. A Tamil man in tattered clothes, head-gear in hand, two front teeth broken and his mouth bleeding, stood before me trembling and weeping. He had been heavily belaboured by his master.

I sent him to a doctor. In those days only white doctors were available. I wanted a certificate from the doctor about the nature of the injury. I secured the certificate, and straightway took the injured man to the magistrate, to whom I submitted his affidavit. The magistrate was indignant when he read it, and issued a summons against the employer. It was far from my desire to get the employer punished. I simply wanted Balasundaram to be released from him.

There were only two ways of releasing Balasundaram: either by getting the Protector of Indentured Labourers to cancel his indenture or transfer him to someone else, or by getting Balasundaram s employer to release him. I called on the latter and said to him: I do not want to proceed against you and get you punished. I shall be satisfied if you will transfer the indenture to someone else. To this he readily agreed. I next saw the Protector. He also agreed, on condition that I found a new employer.

So I went off in search of an employer. At that time I knew very few Europeans. I met one of them. He very kindly agreed to take on Balasundaram. I gratefully acknowledged his kindness. The magistrate convicted Balasundaram s employer, and recorded that he had undertaken to transfer the indenture to someone else. A regular stream of indentured labourers began to pour into my office. The echoes of Balasundaram s case were heard in far off Madras.

In the same year, 1894, the Natal Government sought to impose an annual tax of £ 25 on the indentured Indians. I put the matter before the Congress for discussion, and it was immediately resolved to organize the necessary opposition.

About the year 1860 the Europeans in Natal, finding that there was considerable scope for sugarcane cultivation, felt themselves in need of labour. The Natal Government corresponded with the Indian Government, and secured their permission to recruit Indian labour. These recruits were to sign an indenture to work in Natal for five years, and at the end of the term they were to be at liberty to settle there and to have full rights of ownership of land.

The Indians gave more than had been expected of them. Nor did their enterprise stop at agriculture. They entered trade. They purchased land for building, and many raised themselves from the status of labourers to that of owners of land and houses. Merchants from India followed them and settled there for trade. The white traders were alarmed. This sowed the seed of the antagonism to Indians. Through legislation this antagonism found its expression in the disfranchising bill and the bill to impose a tax.

A deputation composed of Sir Henry Binns and Mr. Mason was sent to India to get the proposal approved by the Government there. The Viceroy at that time was Lord Elgin. He disapproved of the £ 25 tax, but agreed to a poll tax of £ 3. To levy a yearly tax of £ 12 from a family of four when the average income of the husband was never more than 14 s. a month, was atrocious and unknown anywhere else in the world.

We organized a fierce campaign against this tax. If the Natal Indian Congress had remained silent on the subject, the Viceroy might have approved of even the £ 25 tax.

The Congress could not regard it as any great achievement. It ever retained its determination to get the tax remitted, but it was twenty years before the determination was realized.

By now I had been three years in South Africa. In 1896 I asked permission to go home for six months, for I saw that I was in for a long stay there. I had established a fairly good practice, and could see that people felt the need of my presence. So I made up my mind to go home, fetch my wife and children, and then return and settle down there. I also saw that, if I went home, I might be able to do there some public work by educating public opinion and creating more interest in the Indians of South Africa.

About the middle of 1896 I sailed for home in the S.S. Pongola which was bound for Calcutta.

◆◆◆

Gandhi Flowers

'An ounce of practice is worth more than tons of preaching.'

●

5
PROMOTING THE S. AFRICA CAUSE IN INDIA

On my way to Bombay the train stopped at Allahabad and I got down there. I took a room at Kellner s and stayed there. I had heard a good deal about *The Pioneer* published from Allahabad, and I had understood it to be an opponent of Indian aspirations. I had an impression that Mr. Cheseny Jr. was the editor at that time. I wanted to secure the help of every party, so I wrote a note to Mr. Chesney, asking for an appointment. He immediately gave me one, at which I was very happy, especially when I found that he gave me a patient hearing. He promised to notice in his paper anything that I might write, but added that he could not promise to endorse all the Indian demands.

This unexpected interview with the editor of *The Pioneer* laid the foundation of the series of incidents which ultimately led to my being almost lynched in Natal.

I then went straight to Rajkot without halting at Bombay and began to make preparations for writing a pamphlet on the situation in South Africa. The writing and publication of the pamphlet took about a month. Ten thousand copies were printed and sent to all the papers and leaders of every party in India. *The Pioneer* was the first to notice it editorially. A summary of the article was cabled by Reuter to England, and a summary of that summary was cabled to Natal by Reuter s London office. Every paper of note commented at length on the question.

Hardly ever have I known anybody to cherish such loyalty as I did to the British Constitution. The National Anthem used to be sung at every meeting that I attended in Natal. I then felt that I must also join in the singing. **In those days I believed that British rule was on the whole beneficial to the ruled.** I taught the National Anthem to the children of my family. Later on the text began to jar on me. As my conception of ahimsa went on maturing, I became more vigilant about my thought and speech.

Whilst busy in Rajkot with the pamphlet I had an occasion to pay a flying visit to Bombay. First of all I met Justice Ranade, who listened to me with attention, and advised me to meet Sir Pherozeshah Mehta. Justice Badruddin Tyabji, whom I met next, also gave the same advice.

I certainly wanted to see Sir Pherozeshah Mehta. In due course I met him. I was prepared to be awed by his presence. But the king did not overpower me. He met me as a loving father would meet his grown up son. Our meeting took place at his chamber. He was surrounded by a circle of friends and followers. Amongst them were Mr. D. E. Wacha and Mr. Qama, to whom I was introduced. Mr. Wacha said, Gandhi, we must meet again.

Sir Pherozeshah carefully listened to me. Gandhi, said he, I see that I must help you. I must call a public meeting here. With this he turned to Mr. Munshi, the secretary, and told him to fix up the date of the meeting. The interview removed my fears, and I went home delighted.

The meeting was held in the hall of Sir Cowasji Jehangir Institute. This was the first meeting of the kind in my experience. I saw that my voice could reach only a few. **I was trembling as I began to read my speech. Sir Pherozeshah cheered me up continually by asking me to speak louder and still louder.** Sir Pherozeshah liked the speech. I was supremely happy.

From Bombay I went to Poona. First I met ***Lokmanya Tilak***. He said: You are quite right in seeking the help of all parties. But you must have a non-party man for your President. Meet Professor Bhandarkar. See him and let me know what he says. I want to help you to the fullest extent. This was my first meeting with Lokmanya. It revealed to me the secret of his unique popularity.

Next I met **Gokhale**. I found him on the Fergusson College grounds. He gave me an affectionate welcome, and his manner immediately won my heart. **Sir Pherozeshah had seemed to me like the Himalaya, and Lokmanya like the ocean. But Gokhale was as the Ganges. One could have a refreshing bath in the holy river.** Gokhale closely examined me, as a schoolmaster would examine a candidate seeking admission to a school. He told me whom to approach and how to approach them. He assured me that he was always at my disposal.

Dr. Bhandarkar received me with the warmth of a father. My insistence of a non-party man for the president of the meeting had his ready approval. Without any ado this erudite and selfless band of workers in Poona held a meeting in an unostentatious little place, and sent me away rejoicing and more confident of my mission.

I next proceeded to Madras. It was wild with enthusiasm. The Balasundaram incident made a profound impression on the meeting. My speech was printed and was, for me, fairly long. But the audience listened to every word with attention. The greatest help here came to me from the late Sjt. G. Parameshvaran Pillay, the editor of *The Madras Standard.* He placed the columns of *The Madras Standard* entirely at my disposal, and I freely availed myself of the offer.

From Madras I proceeded to Calcutta. I took a room in the Great Eastern Hotel. Here I became acquainted with Mr. Ellerthorpe, a representative of *The Daily Telegraph.* I had of course to see **Surendranath Banerji**, the Idol of Bengal . When I met him, he was surrounded by a number of friends. He said: I am afraid people will not take interest in your work. But you must try as best as you can. You will have to enlist the sympathy of Maharajas. You should meet Raja Sir Pyarimohan Mukerji and

Maharshi Tagore. Both are liberal-minded and take a fair share in public work. I met these gentlemen, but without success. Both gave me a cold reception and said it was no easy thing to call a public meeting in Calcutta.

I called at the office of *The Amrita Bazar Patrika.* **The gentleman whom I met there took me to be a wandering Jew. *The Bangabasi* went even one better. The editor kept me waiting for an hour.** But I was not discouraged. I kept on seeing editors of other papers. As usual I met the Anglo-Indian editors also. *The Statesman* and *The Englishman* realized the importance of the question. I gave them long interviews, and they published them in full.

The unexpected help of Mr. Saunders, editor of *The Englishman* had begun to encourage me to think that I might succeed after all in holding a public meeting in Calcutta, when I received the following cable from Durban: Parliament opens January. Return soon.

Dada Abdulla had just then purchased the steamship *Courland,* and insisted on my travelling on that boat, offering to take me and my family free of charge. I gratefully accepted the offer, and in the beginning of December set sail a second time for South Africa, now with my wife and two sons and the only son of my widowed sister. Another steamship *'Naderi'* also sailed for Durban at the same time.

◆◆◆

6
WITH FAMILY IN S. AFRICA

The two ships cast anchor in the port of Durban on or about the 18th of December. As there had been plague in Bombay when we set sail, we feared that we might have to go through a brief quarantine. The doctor came and examined us. He ordered a five days quarantine.

But this quarantine order had more than health reasons behind it. The white residents of Durban had been agitating for our repatriation, and the agitation was one of the reasons for the order. The whites were holding monster meetings every day. They were addressing all kinds of threats and at times offering even inducements to Dada Abdulla and Co. They were ready to indemnify the Company if both the ships should be sent back. But Dada Abdulla and Co. were not the people to be afraid of threats.

Thus Durban had become the scene of an unequal duel. On one side there was a handful of poor Indians and a few of their English friends, and on the other were ranged the white men, strong in arms, in numbers, in education and in wealth. They had also the backing of the State.

Gandhi, Go Back!

Now threats began to be addressed to us: 'If you do not go back, you will surely be pushed into the sea. But if you consent to return, you may even get your passage money back. I constantly moved amongst my fellow-passengers cheering them up.

I was the real target. **There were two charges against me:**

1. that whilst in India I had indulged in unmerited condemnation of the Natal whites;
2. that with a view to swamping Natal with Indians I had specially brought the two shiploads of passengers to settle there.

Ultimatums were served on the passengers and me. We were asked to submit, if we would escape with our lives. In our reply the passengers and I both maintained our right to land at Port Natal, and intimated our determination to enter Natal at any risk. At the end of 23 days the ships were permitted to enter the harbour, and orders permitting the passengers to land were passed.

So the ships were brought into the dock and the passengers began to go ashore. But Mr. Escombe had sent word to the captain that, as the whites were highly enraged against me and my life was in danger, my family and I should be advised to land at dusk, when the Port Superintendent Mr. Tatum would escort us home. But scarcely half an hour after this Mr. Laughton came to the captain. He said: I would like to take Mr. Gandhi with me. **If you are not afraid, I suggest that Mrs. Gandhi and the children should drive to Mr. Rustomji s house, whilst you and I follow them on foot. I do not like the idea of your entering the city like a thief in the night.** I do not think there is any fear of anyone hurting you. Everything is quiet now. I readily agreed. My wife and children drove safely to Mr. Rustomji s place. I went ashore with Mr. Laughton. Mr. Rustomji s house was about two miles from the dock.

As soon as we landed, some youngsters recognized me and shouted Gandhi, Gandhi . About half a dozen men rushed to the spot and joined in the shouting. Mr. Laughton hailed a rickshaw. But the youngsters would not let me get into it. They frightened the rickshaw-boy out of his life, and he took to his heels. As we went ahead, the crowd continued to swell, until it became impossible to proceed further. They first caught hold of Mr. Laughton and separated us. **Then they pelted me with stones, brickbats and rotten eggs. Someone snatched away my turban, whilst others began to batter and kick me. I fainted and caught hold of the front railings of a house and stood there to get my breath. But it was impossible. They came upon me boxing and battering.** The wife of the Police Superintendent, who knew me, happened to be passing by. The brave lady came up, opened her parasol though there was no sun then, and stood between the crowd and me.

This checked the fury of the mob, as it was difficult for them to deliver blows on me without harming Mrs. Alexander.

Meanwhile, an Indian youth who witnessed the incident had run to the police station. The Police Superintendent Mr. Alexander sent a posse of men to ring me round and escort me safely to my destination. I arrived without further harm at Mr. Rustomji s place. I had bruises all over, but no abrasions except in one place.

The Escape Drama

There was quiet inside, but outside the whites surrounded the house. The yelling crowd was shouting, We must have Gandhi. The quick-sighted Police Superintendent was already there. He sent me a message to this effect: If you would save your friend s house and property and also your family, you should escape from the house in disguise.

I put on an Indian constable s uniform and wore on my head a Madrasi scarf, wrapped round a plate to serve as a helmet. Two detectives accompanied me, one of them disguised as an Indian merchant. We reached a neighbouring shop by a bylane and, making our way through the gunny bags piled in the godown, escaped by the gate of the shop and threaded our way through the crowd to a carriage that had been kept for me at the end of the street.

Whilst I had been thus effecting my escape, Mr. Alexander had kept the crowd amused by singing the tune:

Hang old Gandhi
On the sour apple tree.

When he was informed of my safe arrival at the police station, he thus broke the news to the crowd: Well, your victim has made good his escape through a neighbouring shop. You had better go home now. Some of them were angry, others laughed, some refused to believe the story.

The crowd sent their representatives to search the house. They soon returned with disappointing news, and the crowd broke up at last.

Mr. Chamberlain, who was then Secretary of State for the Colonies, cabled asking the Natal Government to prosecute my assailants. Mr. Escombe sent for me, expressed his regret for the injuries I had sustained, and said: If you can identify the assailants, I am prepared to arrest and prosecute them.

To which I gave the following reply:

I do not want to prosecute anyone. What is the use of getting them punished? I do not hold the assailants to blame. They were given to understand that I had made exaggerated statements in India about the whites in Natal. **The leaders, and, if you will permit me to say so, you are to blame. You could have guided the people properly, but you also believed Reuter and assumed that I must have indulged in exaggeration.** I am sure that, when the truth becomes known, they will be sorry for their conduct.

On the day of landing, a representative of *The Natal Advertiser* had come to interview me. He had asked me a number of questions, and in reply I had been able to refute everyone of the charges that had been levelled against me. Thanks to Sir Pherozeshah Mehta, I had delivered only written speeches in India, and I had copies of them all, as well. I had given the interviewer all this literature and showed him that in India.

This interview and my refusal to prosecute the assailants produced such a profound impression that the Europeans of Durban were ashamed of their conduct. The press declared me to be innocent and condemned the mob. **Thus the lynching ultimately proved to be a blessing for me, that is, for the cause. It enhanced the prestige of the Indian community in South Africa and made my work easier.**

In three or four days I went to my house, and it was not long before I settled down again. The incident added also to my professional practice. But if it enhanced the prestige of the community, it also fanned the flame of prejudice against it. As soon as it was proved that the Indian could put up a manly fight, he came to be regarded as a danger. Two bills were introduced in the Natal Legislative Assembly, one of them calculated to affect the Indian trader adversely, and the other to impose a stringent restriction on Indian immigration. Fortunately, the fight for the franchise had resulted in a decision, that is to say, that the law should make no distinctions of colour or race.

The bills considerably increased my public work. We appealed to the Colonial Secretary, but he refused to interfere and the bills became law.

Serving in the Boer War : A New Idea

When the Boer war was declared, my personal sympathies were all with the Boers, but I believed then that I had yet no right in such cases to enforce my individual convictions. My loyalty to the British rule drove me to participation with the British in that war. **I felt that, if I demanded rights as a British citizen, it was also my duty as such, to participate in the defence of the British Empire. I held then that India could achieve her emancipation only within and through the British Empire.** So I collected together as many comrades as possible, and with great difficulty got their services accepted as an ambulance corps.

We secured medical certificates of fitness for service. Mr. Laughton and Mr. Escombe enthusiastically supported the plan. The Boers had shown more pluck, determination and bravery than had been expected; and our services were ultimately needed.

Our corps was 1,100 strong, with nearly 40 leaders. About three hundred were free Indians, and the rest indentured. The authorities did not want us to be within the range of fire. The situation, however, was changed after the repulse at Spion Kop. General Buller sent the message that the

Government would be thankful if we would fetch the wounded from the field. During these days we had to march from twenty to twenty-five miles a day, bearing the wounded on stretchers.

Our humble work was at the moment much applauded, and the Indians prestige was enhanced. General Buller mentioned with appreciation the work of the corps in his despatch, and the leaders were awarded the War Medal. The whites during the war were of the sweetest. We had come in contact with thousands of tommies.

Ever since my settlement in Natal, I had been endeavouring to clear the community of a charge that had been levelled against it, that the Indian was slovenly in his habits and did not keep his house and surroundings clean. House-to-house inspection was undertaken when plague was reported to be imminent in Durban. But I saw that I could not so easily count on the help of the community in getting it to do its own duty, as I could in claiming for its rights. At some places I met with insults, at others with polite indifference. It was too much for people to bestir themselves to keep their surroundings clean.

On my relief from war-duty I felt that my work was no longer in South Africa but in India. Friends at home were also pressing me to return. And for the work in South Africa, there were, of course, Messrs Khan and Mansukhlal Naazar. So I requested my co-workers to relieve me. After very great difficulty my request was conditionally accepted, the condition being that I should be ready to go back to South Africa if, within a year, the community should need me.

◆◆◆

7
ENTERING THE CONGRESS IN INDIA
Age 32

I sailed for home. Mauritius was one of the ports of call, and as the boat made a long halt there, I went ashore and acquainted myself fairly well with the local conditions. For one night I was the guest of Sir Charles Bruce, the Governor of the Colony.

After reaching India I spent some time in going about the country. It was the year 1901 when the Congress met at Calcutta under the presidentship of Mr. Dinshaw Wacha. And I of course attended it. It was my first experience of the Congress.

From Bombay I travelled in the same train as Sir Pherozeshah Mehta. As soon as he saw me, he said, Gandhi, it seems nothing can be done for you. Of course we will pass the resolution you want. But what rights have we in our own country? I believe that, so long as we have no power in our own land, you cannot fare better in the Colonies.

I was taken aback. Mr. Setalvad seemed to concur in the view, Mr. Wacha cast a pathetic look at me. You will of course show me the resolution, said Mr. Wacha, to cheer me up.

At Congress Session 1901

We reached Calcutta. The President was taken to his camp with great eclat by the Reception Committee. I asked a volunteer where I was to go. He took me to Ripon College, where a number of delegates were being put up. Fortune favoured me. Lokmanya was put up in the same block as I.

And as was natural, Lokmanya would never be without his darbar. Were I a painter, I could paint him as I saw him seated on his bed so vivid is the whole scene in my memory. Their loud laughter and their talks about the wrongdoings of the ruling race cannot be forgotten.

In this camp the volunteers were clashing against one another. You asked one of them to do something. He delegated it to another, and he in his turn to a third, and so on. I made friends with a few volunteers. I told them something about South Africa, and they felt somewhat ashamed. The Congress would meet three days every year and then go to sleep. And the delegates were of a piece with the volunteers. They would do nothing themselves. Volunteer, do this, Volunteer, do that, were their constant orders.

Here **I was face to face with untouchability in a fair measure. The Tamilian kitchen was far away from the rest. To the Tamil delegates even the sight of others, whilst they were dining, meant pollution.** So a special kitchen had to be made for them in the College compound, walled in by wickerwork. It was full of smoke which choked you. It was a kitchen, dining room, washroom, all in one a closet safe with no outlet. To me this looked like a travesty of Varna Dharma.

There was no limit to insanitation. Pools of water were everywhere. There were only a few latrines, and the recollection of their stink still oppresses me. I pointed it out to the volunteers. They said pointblank: That is not our work, it is the scavenger s work. **I asked for a broom. The man stared at me in wonder. I procured one and cleaned the latrine.** I saw that, **if the Congress session were to be prolonged, conditions would be quite favourable for the outbreak of an epidemic.**

There were yet two days for the Congress session to begin. So as soon as I had finished the daily ablutions on arrival at Calcutta, I proceeded to the Congress office.

Babu Bhupendranath Basu and Sjt. Ghosal were the secretaries. I went to Bhupen Babu and offered my services. He looked at me, and said: I have no work, but possibly Ghosal Babu might have something to give you.

He scanned me and said with a smile: I can give you only clerical work. Will you do it?

Certainly, said I. I am here to do anything that is not beyond my capacity.

That is the right spirit, young man, he said.

Well then, here is a heap of letters for disposal. Take that chair and begin. Most of these letters have nothing in them, but you will please look them through. Acknowledge those that are worth it, and refer to me those that need a considered reply.

I found my work very easy I had done with it in no time, and Sjt. Ghosal was very glad. He was talkative. He would talk away for hours together. **When he learnt something from me about my history, he felt rather sorry to have given me clerical work.** But I reassured him: Please don t worry. What am I before you? You have grown gray in the service of the Congress, and are as an elder to me. You have put me under a debt of obligation by entrusting me with this work. For I want to do Congress work, and you have given me the rare opportunity of understanding the details.

Sjt. Ghosal used to get his shirt buttoned by his bearer. I volunteered to do the bearer s duty, and I loved to do it. **Asking me to button his shirt, he would say, You see now, the Congress secretary has no time even to button his shirt.** He has always some work to do.

In a few days I came to know the working of the Congress. I met most of the leaders. I also noticed the huge waste of time there. I observed, too, the prominent place that the English language occupied in our affairs. There was little regard for economy of energy.

In the Congress at last. The immense pavilion and the volunteers in stately array, as also the elders seated on the dais, overwhelmed me. The presidential address was a book by itself. To read it from cover to cover was out of the question. Only a few passages were therefore read. After this came the election of the Subjects Committee. Gokhale took me to the Committee meetings.

Sir Pherozeshah had of course agreed to admit my resolution, but I was wondering who would put it before the Subjects Committee, and when. For there were lengthy speeches to every resolution, all in English to boot, and every resolution had some well-known leader to back it. Mine was but a feeble pipe amongst those veteran drums, and as the night was closing in, my heart beat fast. It was 11 o clock. I had not the courage to speak. **I had already met Gokhale, who had looked at my resolution. So I drew near his chair and whispered to him: Please do something for me.**

So we have done? said Sir Pherozeshah Mehta.

No, no, there is still the resolution on South Africa. Mr. Gandhi has been waiting long, cried out Gokhale.

Have you seen the resolution? asked Sir Pherozeshah.

Of course.

Do you like it?

It is quite good.

Well then, let us have it, Gandhi.

I read it trembling. Gokhale supported it.

Unanimously passed, cried out everyone.

You will have five minutes to speak, Gandhi, said Mr. Wacha.

The morning had found me worrying about my

speech. What was I to say in five minutes? I had prepared myself fairly well, but the words would not come to me. I had decided not to read my speech but to speak extempore. **But the facility for speaking that I had acquired in South Africa seemed to have left me for the moment.**

As soon as Mr. Wacha called out my name, I stood up. **My head was reeling. I read the resolution somehow.** Someone had printed and distributed amongst the delegates copies of a poem he had written in praise of foreign emigration. I read the poem and referred to the grievances of the settlers in South Africa.

Just at this moment Mr. Wacha rang the bell. I did not know that the bell was rung in order to warn me to finish in two minutes more. I sat down as soon as the bell was rung. Everyone raised his hand and all resolutions were passed unanimously.

The Congress was over, but as I had to meet the Chamber of Commerce and various people in connection with work in South Africa, I stayed in Calcutta for a month. I arranged to get the required introduction for a room in the India Club. Among its members were some prominent Indians, and I looked forward to getting into touch with them and interesting them in the work in South Africa. Gokhale frequently went to this Club to play billiards, and when he knew that I was to stay in Calcutta for some time, he invited me to stay with him. He said. Gandhi, you have to stay in the country and I want you to do Congress work.

From the very first day of my stay with him Gokhale made me feel completely at home. He treated me as though I were his younger brother. To see Gokhale at work was as much a joy as an education. He never wasted a minute. His private relations and friendships were all for public good. India s poverty and subjection were matters of constant and intense concern to him.

During these days I walked up and down the streets of Calcutta. I went to most places on foot. I met Justice Mitter and Sir Gurudas Banerji and Raja Pyarimohan Mukerji.

At Kali Temple

Kalicharan Banerji had spoken to me about the Kali temple, which I was eager to see. So I went there one day. On the way I saw a stream of sheep going to be sacrificed to Kali. Rows of beggars lined the lane leading to the temple. There were religious mendicants too, and **even in those days I was sternly opposed to giving alms to sturdy beggars.** One of such men stopped me and accosted me: 'Whither are you going, my boy?

I asked him: Do you regard this sacrifice as religion?

Who would regard killing of animals as religion?

Then, why don t you preach against it?

That s not my business. Our business is to worship God.

But could you not find any other place in which to worship God?

All places are equally good for us. The people are like a flock of sheep, following where leaders lead them. It is no business of us *sadhus.'*

We did not prolong the discussion but passed on to the temple. We were greeted by rivers of blood. I could not bear to stand there. I was exasperated and restless. **I have never forgotten that sight.**

That very evening I had an invitation to dinner at a party of Bengali friends. There I spoke to a friend about this cruel form of worship. He said: The sheep don t feel anything. The noise and the drumbeating there deaden all sensation of pain.

I could not swallow this. **I felt that the cruel custom ought to be stopped but I also saw that the task was beyond my capacity.**

I hold today the same opinion as I held then. To my mind the life of a lamb is no less precious than that of a human being. How is it that Bengal with all its knowledge, intelligence, sacrifice, and emotion tolerates this slaughter?

The terrible sacrifice offered to Kali in the name of religion enhanced my desire to know Bengali life. I had read and heard a good deal about the Brahmo Samaj. I met Pandit Shivanath Shastri and in company with Prof. Kathavate went to see Maharshi Devendranath Tagore, but as no interviews with him were allowed then, we could not see him.

It was impossible to be satisfied without seeing Swami Vivekanand. So with great enthusiasm **I**

went to Belur Math, mostly, or maybe all the way, on foot. I loved the sequestered site of the Math. I was disappointed and sorry to be told that the Swami was at his Calcutta house, lying ill, and could not be seen.

I then ascertained the place of residence of Sister Nivedita, and met her in a Chowringhee mansion. I was taken aback by the splendour that surrounded her, and even in our conversation there was not much meeting ground. I spoke to Gokhale about this, and he said he did not wonder that there could be no point of contact between me and a volatile person like her.

I met her again at Mr. Pestonji Padshah s place. I happened to come in just as she was talking to his old mother, and so I became an interpreter between the two. In spite of my failure to find any agreement with her, I could not but notice and admire her overflowing love for Hinduism.

I must needs skip over many a reminiscence of this memorable month. Let me simply mention my flying visit to Burma, and the *foongis* (monks) there. **I was pained by their lethargy. I saw the golden pagoda. I did not like the innumerable little candles burning in the temple, and the rats running about the sanctum** brought to my mind thoughts of Swami Dayanand s experience at Morvi.

Touring India

Before settling down I had thought of making a tour through India travelling third class, and of acquainting myself with the hardships of third class passengers. I spoke to Gokhale about this. To begin with, he ridiculed the idea, but when I explained to him what I hoped to see, he cheerfully approved. I planned to go first to Benares to pay my respects to Mrs. Besant, who was then ill.

It was necessary to equip myself anew for the third class tour. Gokhale himself gave me a metal tiffin-box and got it filled with sweet balls and *puris.* I purchased a canvas bag worth twelve annas and a long coat made of coarse Chhaya wool. The bag was to contain this coat, a *dhoti,* a towel and a shirt. I had a blanket as well to cover myself with and a water jug. Thus equipped I set forth on my travels. Gokhale and Dr. P.C. Ray came to the station to see me off. I had asked them both not to trouble to come, but they insisted. I should not have come if you had gone first class, but now I had to, said Gokhale.

The journey was from Calcutta to Rajkot, and I planned to halt at Benares, Agra, Jaipur and Palanpur en route.

I arrived in Benares in the morning. I had decided to put up with a *panda.* Numerous Brahmins surrounded me, as soon as I got out of the train, and I selected one who struck me to be comparatively cleaner and better than the rest. There was a cow in the courtyard of his house and an upper storey where I was given a lodging. I did not want to have any food without ablution in the Ganges in the proper orthodox manner. The *panda* made preparations for it.

The *puja* was over at twelve o clock and I went to the Kashi Vishvanath temple for *darshan*. I was deeply pained by what I saw there. The approach was through a narrow and slippery lane. The swarming flies and the noise made by the shop-keepers and pilgrims were perfectly insufferable. Where one expected an atmosphere of meditation and communion, it was conspicuous by its absence. When I reached the temple, I was greeted at the entrance by a stinking mass of rotten flowers.

I went near the Jnana-vapi (Well of Knowledge). **I searched here for God but failed to find Him.** The surroundings of the Jnana-vapi too I found to be dirty. I had no mind to give any *dakshina*. So I offered a pie. The *panda* in charge got angry and threw away the pie. **He swore at me and said, This insult will take you straight to hell.'**

Maharaj , said I, whatever fate has in store for me, it does not behove one of your class to indulge in such language. You may take this pie if you like, or you will lose that too.

Go away, he replied, I don t care for your pie. And then followed a further volley of abuse.

I took up the pie and went my way. But the Maharaj called me back and said, All right, leave it, if I refuse your pie, it will be bad for you.

I silently gave him the pie and, with a sigh, went away.

After this visit, I waited upon Mrs. Besant.

I knew that she had just recovered from an illness. I sent in my name. She came at once. As I wished only to pay my respects to her, I said, I only wanted to pay my respects. I am thankful that you have been good enough to receive me in spite of your indifferent health. I will not detain you any longer. So saying, I took leave of her.

Gokhale was very anxious that I should settle down in Bombay, practise at the bar and help him in public work. Public work in those days meant Congress work, and the chief work of the institution which he had assisted to found was carrying on the Congress administration.

I liked Gokhale s advice, but I was not overconfident of success as a barrister. The unpleasant memories of past failure were yet with me. I took chambers in Payne, Gilbert and Sayani s offices, and it looked as though I had settled down.

I had a house in Girgaum, but the house was not habitable. It was damp and ill-lighted. So I decided to hire some well-ventilated bungalow in a suburb of Bombay. I wandered about in Bandra and Santa Cruz. The slaughter house in Bandra prevented our choice falling there. Ghatkopar and places near it were too far from the sea. At last we hit upon a fine bungalow in Santa Cruz.

I took a first class season ticket from Santa Cruz to Churchgate, and remember having frequently felt a certain pride in being the only first class passenger in my compartment. Often I walked to Bandra in order to take the fast train from there direct to Churchgate. I prospered in my profession better than I had expected.

Just when I seemed to be settling down as I had intended, I received an unexpected cable from South Africa: Chamberlain expected here. Please return immediately.

I reached Durban not a day too soon. There was work waiting for me. The date for the deputation to wait on Mr. Chamberlain had been fixed. I had to draft the memorial to be submitted to him and accompany the deputation.

◆◆◆

Gandhi Flowers

'A good thought is like fragrance.'

●

8
AGAIN IN SOUTH AFRICA

Mr. Chamberlain had come to get a gift of 35 million pounds from South Africa, and to win the hearts of Englishmen and Boers. So he gave a cold shoulder to the Indian deputation.

You know, he said, that the Imperial Government has little control over self-governing colonies. Your grievances seem to be genuine. I shall do what I can, but you must try your best to placate the Europeans, if you wish to live in their midst.

The reply cast a chill over the members of the deputation. I was also disappointed. It was an eye-opener for us all, and I saw that we should start with our work *de novo.*

From Natal he hastened to the Transvaal. I had to prepare the case for the Indians there as well and submit it to him. But how was I to get to Pretoria? Our people there were not in a position to procure the necessary legal facilities for my getting to them in time. The War had reduced the Transvaal to a howling wilderness. Every Transvaaller had therefore to obtain a permit.

During the War many officers and soldiers had

come to South Africa from India and Ceylon, and it was considered to be the duty of the British authorities to provide for such of them as decided to settle there. The quick ingenuity of some of them created a new department. There was a special department for the Negroes. Why then should there not be one for the Asiatics? When I reached the Transvaal, this new department had already been opened and was gradually spreading its tentacles.

The Indians had to apply to this department. A reply would be vouchsafed many days after. And as there were large numbers wishing to return to the Transvaal, there grew up an army of intermediaries or touts, who, with the officers, looted the poor Indians to the tune of thousands. I was told that no permit could be had without influence, and that in some cases one had to pay up to hundred pounds in spite of the influence. I went to my old friend, the Police Superintendent of Durban, and said to him: Please introduce me to the Permit Officer and help me to obtain a permit. He immediately put on his hat, came out and secured me a permit. I thanked Superintendent Alexander and started for Pretoria.

On reaching Pretoria I drafted the memorial.

The officers at the head of the new department were at a loss to know how I had entered the Transvaal. They only ventured a guess that I might have succeeded in entering without a permit on the strength of my old connections. If that was the case, I was liable to be arrested!

The officers sent telegrams to Durban, and when they found that I had entered with a permit, they were disappointed. But they were not the men to be defeated by such disappointment. They could still successfully prevent me from waiting on Mr. Chamberlain.

So the community was asked to submit the names of the representatives who were to form the Deputation. I was first summoned to see the chief of the department, an officer from Ceylon.

What brings you here? said the Sahib addressing me.

I have come here at the request of my fellow countrymen to help them with my advice, I replied.

But don t you know that you have no right to come here? The permit you hold was given you by mistake. You cannot be regarded as a domiciled Indian. You must go back. You shall not wait on Mr. Chamberlain. Well, you may go. With this he bade me good-bye, giving me no opportunity for a reply. But he detained my companions. He gave them a sound scolding and advised them to send me away.

I was fully conscious of the limitations of the community. I pacified my friends and advised them to have, in my place, Mr. George Godfrey, an Indian barrister. So Mr. Godfrey led the deputation. Mr. Chamberlain referred in his reply to my exclusion. Rather than hear the same representative over and over again, is it not better to have someone new? he said, and tried to heal the wound.

But all this, far from ending the matter, only added to the work of the community and also to mine. We had to start afresh. So I set the ball rolling, discussed things with Indians in Pretoria and Johannesburg, and ultimately decided to set up office in Johannesburg.

It was indeed doubtful whether I would be enrolled in the Transvaal Supreme Court. But the Law Society did not oppose my application and the Court allowed it. I succeeded in securing suitable rooms for my office in the legal quarters of the city, and I started on my professional work.

Johannesburg was the stronghold of the Asiatic officers. I had been observing that, far from protecting the Indians, Chinese and others, these officers were grinding them down. Every day I had complaints like this: The rightful ones are not admitted, whilst those who have no right are smuggled in on payment of £ 100. If you will not remedy this state of things, who will?

So I began to collect evidence, and as soon as I had gathered a fair amount, I approached the Police Commissioner. He appeared to be a just man. He examined the witnesses himself and was satisfied, but he knew as well as I that it was difficult in South Africa to get a white jury to convict a white offender against coloured men. But, said he, let us try at any rate. It is not proper either, to let such criminals go scotfree for fear of the jury acquitting them. I must get them arrested.

I suspected quite a number of officers, but as I had no unchallengeable evidence against them all, warrants of arrest were issued against the two about whose guilt I had not the slightest doubt.

One of these absconded. The Police Commissioner obtained an extradition warrant against him and got him arrested and brought to the Transvaal. They were tried, and although there was strong evidence against them, both were declared to be not guilty and acquitted.

However, the guilt of both these officers was so patent that the Government could not harbour them. Both were cashiered, and the Asiatic Department became comparatively clean and the Indian community was somewhat reassured. The event enhanced my prestige and brought me more business. The bulk, though not all, of the hundreds of pounds that the community was monthly squandering in speculation, was saved.

I must say that, though these officers were so bad, I had nothing against them personally. They had a chance of getting employed by the Johannesburg Municipality in case I did not oppose the proposal. A friend of theirs saw me in this connection and I agreed not to thwart them, and they succeeded.

I was not then quite conscious that such behaviour was part of my nature. I learnt later that it was an essential part of Satyagraha, and an attribute of ahimsa.

Starting *Indian Opinion*

About this time Sjt. Madanjit approached me

with a proposal to start *Indian Opinion* and sought my advice. He had already been conducting a press, and I approved of his proposal. The journal was launched in 1904, and Sjt. Mansukhlal Naazar became the first editor. But I had to bear the brunt of the work, having for most of the time to be practically in charge of the journal.

I had no notion that I should have to invest any money in this journal, but I soon discovered that it could not go on without my financial help. I remember a time when I had to remit £ 75 each month. But after all these years I feel that the journal has served the community well. *Indian Opinion* in those days, was a mirror of a part of my life. Week after week I poured out my soul in its columns, and expounded the principles and practice of Satyagraha as I understood it. Satyagraha would probably have been impossible without *Indian Opinion*.

In South Africa we have acquired the odious name of coolies . It means what a pariah or an untouchable means to us, and the quarters assigned to the coolies are known as coolie locations . Johannesburg had one such location, where the Indians had acquired their plots on a lease of 99 years. People were densely packed in the location, Beyond arranging to clean the latrines in the location in a haphazard way, the Municipality did nothing to provide any sanitary facilities, much less good roads or lights. The Municipality used the insanitation as a pretext for destroying the location, and for that purpose obtained from the local legislative authority to dispossess the settlers.

The settlers, having proprietary rights in their land, were naturally entitled to compensation. A special tribunal was appointed to try the land acquisition cases. If the tenant was not prepared to accept the offer of the Municipality, he had a right to appeal to the tribunal, and if the latter s award exceeded the Municipality s offer, the Municipality had to bear the costs.

Most of the tenants engaged me as their legal adviser. I told the tenants that I should be satisfied with whatever costs the tribunal awarded, in case they won, and a fee of £ 10 on every lease, irrespective of the result of the case. I also told them that I proposed to set apart half of the money paid by them for the building of a hospital or similar institution for the poor. This naturally pleased them all.

Out of about 70 cases only one was lost.

The Black Plague

While the Indians were fretting over this state of things, there was a sudden outbreak of the black plague.

Fortunately, it was not the location but one of the gold mines in the vicinity of Johannesburg that was responsible for the outbreak. The workers in this mine were for the most part Negroes. There were a few Indians also working, twenty-three of whom suddenly caught the infection, and returned one evening to their quarters in the location. Sjt.

Madanjit, who was then canvassing subscribers for *Indian Opinion* and realizing subscriptions, happened to be in the location at this moment. He was a remarkably fearless man, and he sent a pencil-note to me to the following effect: There has been a sudden outbreak of the black plague. Please come immediately.

Sjt. Madanjit bravely broke open the lock of a vacant house, and put all the patients there. I cycled to the location. Dr. William Godfrey, who was practising in Johannesburg, ran to the rescue as soon as he got the news, I had at that time four Indians in my office I decided to sacrifice all four.

We pulled all the patients through that night! The next day they placed a vacant godown at my disposal. We cleaned it up ourselves, and improvised a temporary hospital. The Municipality lent the services of a nurse, who came with brandy and other hospital equipment.

We had instructions to give the patients frequent doses of brandy. But none of us would touch it. I put three patients, who were prepared to do without brandy, under the earth treatment, applying wet earth bandages to their heads and chests. Two of these were saved. The other twenty died in the godown.

I had addressed a strong letter to the press, holding the Municipality guilty of negligence after the location came into its possession and responsible for the outbreak of the plague itself.

I used to have my meals at a vegetarian

restaurant. Here I met Mr. Albert West. Mr. West was a partner in a small printing concern. He read my letter in the press about the outbreak of the plague and, not finding me in the restaurant for a day or two, knocked at my door early one morning. I did not find you in the restaurant and was really afraid lest something should have happened to you; so I decided to come and see you. I am ready to help in nursing the patients.

I expressed my gratitude, and without taking even a second to think, replied: I will not have you as a nurse. If there are no more cases, we shall be free in a day or two. There is one thing however.

Yes, what is it?

'Could you take charge of the *Indian Opinion* press at Durban? Mr. Madanjit is likely to be engaged here, and someone is needed at Durban.

You know that I have a press. Most probably I shall be able to go, but may I give my final reply in the evening?

I was delighted. We had the talk. He agreed to go. Salary was no consideration to him, as money was not his motive. But a salary of £ 10 per month and a part of the profits, if any, was fixed up. The very next day Mr. West left for Durban by the evening mail. From that day until the time I left the shores of South Africa, he remained a partner of my joys and sorrows.

I made the acquaintance of Mr. Polak in the vegetarian restaurant. One evening a young man dining at a table a little way off sent me his card expressing a desire to see me. I invited him to come to my table.

I am sub-editor of *The Critic,'* he said. When I read your letter to the press about the plague, I felt a strong desire to see you.

Mr. Polak s candour drew me to him. We seemed to hold closely similar views on the essential things of life. He liked simple life. He had a wonderful faculty of translating into practice anything that appealed to his intellect.

Indian Opinion was getting more and more expensive every day. The very first report from Mr. West was alarming.

I left for Natal. I had taken Mr. Polak into my fullest confidence. He came to see me off at the station, and left with me a book to read during the journey, which he said I was sure to like. It was Ruskin s *Unto This Last.*

The book was impossible to lay aside, once I had begun it. It was the one that brought about an instantaneous and practical transformation in my life. I translated it later into Gujarati, entitling it *Sarvodaya* (the welfare of all).

The Phoenix Settlement

I talked over the whole thing with Mr. West, described to him the effect *Unto This Last* had produced on my mind, and proposed that *Indian Opinion* should be removed to a farm, on which everyone should labour, drawing the same living wage, and attending to the press work in spare time. Mr. West approved of the proposal, and £ 3 was laid down as the monthly allowance per head, irrespective of colour or nationality.

I talked to the workers on the terms of this proposal. It did not appeal to Sjt. Madanjit, who held that it would ruin a venture on which he had staked his all.

Among the men working in the press was Chhaganlal Gandhi, one of my cousins. He had a wife and children, but he had from childhood chosen to be trained and to work under me. So without any argument he agreed to the scheme. The machinist Govindaswami also fell in with the proposal. The rest did not join the scheme, but agreed to go wherever I removed the press.

Thereafter I at once advertised for a piece of land situated near a railway station in the vicinity of Durban. An offer came in respect of Phoenix. Mr. West and I went to inspect the estate. Within a week we purchased twenty acres of land. It had a nice little spring and a few orange and mango trees. Adjoining it was a piece of 80 acres which had many more fruit trees and a dilapidated cottage. We purchased this too, the total cost being a thousand pounds.

Mr. Rustomji placed at my disposal second-hand corrugated iron sheets of a big godown and other building material. Some Indian carpenters and masons, who had worked with me in the Boer War, helped me in erecting a shed for the press. At first we all lived under canvas. We carted most of our things to Phoenix in about a week.

It was no easy thing to issue the first number of *Indian Opinion* from Phoenix. The size of the paper, that of a daily, was considered unsuitable for an out-of-the-way place like Phoenix. It was reduced to foolscap size, so that, in case of emergency, copies might be struck off with the help of a treadle.

In the initial stages, we all had to keep late hours before the day of publication. Everyone, young and old, had to help in folding the sheets. We usually finished our work between ten o clock and midnight.

In order to enable everyone of us to make a living by manual labour, we parcelled out the land round the press in pieces of three acres each. One of these fell to my lot. On all these plots we, much against our wish, built houses with corrugated iron. Our desire had been to have mud huts thatched with straw or small brick houses but it could not be. They would have been more expressive and would have meant more time, and everyone was eager to settle down as soon as possible.

Though we had paid compositors, the idea was for every member of the Settlement to learn typesetting, who did not already know the work learnt it. I remained a dunce to the last.

I informed Polak of the important changes I had made. His joy knew no bounds when he learnt that the loan of his book had been so fruitful. Is it not possible, he asked, for me to take part in the new venture? Certainly. I am quite ready, he replied, if you will admit me.

He gave a month s notice to his chief to be relieved from *The Critic,* and reached Phoenix in due course. By his sociability he won the hearts of all and soon became a member of the family. But I could not keep him there long. Mr. Ritch had decided to finish his legal studies in England, and it was impossible for me to bear the burden of the office singlehanded, so I suggested to Polak that he should join the office and qualify as an attorney. Polak left Phoenix, came to Johannesburg and signed his articles with me.

Thus, with the laudable object of quickly realizing the ideals at Phoemx, I seemed to be going deeper and deeper into a contrary current, and had God not willed otherwise, I should have found myself entrapped in this net spread in the name of simple life.

I had now given up all hope of returning to India in the near future. I had promised my wife that I would return home within a year. The year was gone without any prospect of my return, so I decided to send for her and the children.

Just when I felt that I should be breathing in peace, an unexpected event happened. The papers brought the news of the outbreak of the Zulu rebellion in Natal. I bore no grudge against the Zulus, they had harmed no Indian. I had doubts about the rebellion itself. But I then believed that the British Empire existed for the welfare of the world. Natal had a Volunteer Defence Force, and was open to it to recruit more men. I read that this force had already been mobilized to quell the rebellion .

I considered myself a citizen of Natal, being intimately connected with it. So I wrote to the Governor, expressing my readiness, if necessary, to form an Indian Ambulance Corps. He replied immediately accepting the offer.

I went to Durban and appealed for men. A big contingent was not necessary. We were a party of twenty-four, of whom, besides me, four were Gujaratis. The rest were ex-indentured men from South India.

Sergeant-Major Gandhi

The Chief Medical Officer appointed me to the temporary rank of Sergeant-Major and three men selected by me to the rank of sergeants and one to that of corporal. We also received our uniforms from the Government. Our Corps was on active service for nearly six weeks.

On reaching the scene of the rebellion , I saw that there was nothing there to justify the name of rebellion'. There was no resistance that one could see. The reason why the disturance had been magnified into a rebellion was that a Zulu chief had advised non-payment of a new tax imposed on his people, and had assaulted a sergeant who had gone to collect the tax.

The Medical Officer in charge welcomed us. He said the white people were not willing nurses for the wounded Zulus, that their wounds were festering, and that he was at his wits end. He hailed our arrival as a godsend for those innocent people, and he equipped us with bandages, disinfectants etc., and took us to the improvised hospital. The Zulus were delighted to see us. The white soldiers used to peep through the railings that separated us from them and tried to dissuade us from attending to the wounds.

Gradually I came into closer touch with these soldiers, and they ceased to interfere. Among the commanding officers were Col. Sparks and Col. Wylie, who had bitterly opposed me in 1896. They were surprised at my attitude and specially called and thanked me. They introduced me to General Mackenzie.

Besides this work I had to compound and dispense prescriptions for the white soldiers. This was easy enough for me as I had received a year s training in Dr. Booth s little hospital. This work brought me in close contact with many Europeans.

The Zulu rebellion was full of new experiences and gave me much food for thought. The Boer War had not brought home to me the horrors of war with anything like the vividness that the rebellion did. This was no war but a man-hunt, not only in my opinion, but also in that of many Englishmen with whom I had occasion to talk.

But there was much else to set one thinking. It was a sparsely populated part of the country. Few and far between in hills and dales were the scattered Kraals of the simple and so-called uncivilized Zulus.

Marching, with or without the wounded, through there solemn solitudes, I often fell into deep thought.

Brahmacharya

I pondered over *brahmacharya* and its implications, and my convictions took deep root. It was borne in upon me that I should have more and more occasions for service of the kind I was rendering, and that I should find myself unequal to my task if I were engaged in the pleasures of family life and in the propagation and rearing of children.

On the present occasion, for instance, I should not have been able to throw myself into the fray, had my wife been expecting a baby. Without the observance of *brahmacharya* service of the family would be inconsistent with service of the community. So thinking, I became somewhat impatient to take a final vow.

On my arrival at Phoenix I eagerly broached the subject of *brahmacharya* with Chhaganlal, Maganlal, West and others. They liked the idea and accepted the necessity of taking the vow, but they also presented the difficulties of the task. Some of them set themselves bravely to observe it, and some, I know, succeeded also.

I too took the plunge the vow to observe brahmacharya for life.

The Birth of Satyagraha

Events were so shaping themselves in Johannesburg as to make this self-purification on my part a preliminary as it were to Satyagraha. The principle called Satyagraha came into being before that name was invented.

Indeed when it was born, I myself could not say what it was. In Gujarati also we used the English phrase passive resistance to describe it. When in a meeting of Europeans I found that the term passive resistance was too narrowly construed, that it was supposed to be a weapon of the weak, that it could be characterized by hatred, and that it could finally manifest itself as violence, I had to demur to all these statements and explain the real nature of the Indian movement. It was clear that a new word must be coined by the Indians to designate their struggle.

But I could not for the life of me find out a new name, and therefore offered a nominal prize through *Indian Opinion* to the reader who made the best suggestion on the subject. As a result Maganlal Gandhi coined the word Sadagraha (Sat = truth, Agraha = firmness) and won the prize. But in order to make it clearer I changed the word to Satyagraha . The history of this struggle is for all practical purposes a history of the remainder of my life in South Africa and especially of my experiments with truth in that sub-continent.

Kasturbai s illness during this period was instrumental in bringing about some changes in my diet. The first of these was the giving up of milk. It was from Raychandbhai that I first learnt that milk stimulated animal passion. Books on vegetarianism strengthened the idea. While the necessity for avoiding milk in the interests of self-restraint was growing upon me, I happened to come across some literature from Calcutta, describing the tortures to which cows and buffaloes were subjected by their keepers. This had a wonderful effect on me. I discussed it with Mr. Kallenbach.

Mr. Kallenbach said, We constantly talk about the harmful effects of milk. Why then do not we give it up? It is certainly not necessary. I was agreeably surprised at the suggestion, which I warmly welcomed, and both of us pledged ourselves to abjure milk there and then. This was at Tolstoy Farm in the year 1912.

But this denial was not enough to satisfy me. Soon after this I decided to live on a pure fruit diet, and that too composed of the cheapest fruit possible. Our ambition was to live the life of the poorest people.

I then commenced fasting as a means of self-restraint. When I started on this experiment, the Hindu month of Shravan and the Islamic month of Ramzan happened to coincide. I persuaded the Muslim youngsters to observe the Ramzan fast. I had of course decided to observe *pradosha* myself, but I now asked the Hindu, Parsi and Christian youngsters to join me The result of these experiments was that all were convinced of the value of fasting, and a splendid *esprit de corps* grew up among them.

As the Farm grew, it was found necessary to make some provision for the education of its boys and girls. I had always given the first place to the culture of the heart or the building of character, and as I felt confident that moral training could be given to all alike, no matter how different their ages and their upbringing, I decided to live amongst them all the twenty-four hours of the day as their father. But as I fully appreciated the necessity of a literary training in addition, I started some classes with the help of Mr. Kallenbach and Sjt. Pragji Desai. Nor did I underrate the building up of the body. This they got in the course of their daily routine. For there were no servants on the Farm, and all the work, from cooking down to scavenging, was done by the inmates. There were many fruit trees to be looked after, and enough gardening to be done as well.

It was my intention to teach every one of the youngsters some useful manual vocation. For this purpose Mr. Kallenbach went to a Trappist monastery and returned having learnt shoemaking. I learnt it from him and taught the art to such as were ready to take it up. Mr. Kallenbach had some experience of carpentry, and there was another inmate who knew it; so we had a small class in carpentry. Cooking almost all the youngsters knew.

The spiritual training of the boys was a much more difficult matter than their physical and mental training. I made the children memorize and recite hymns, and read to them from books on moral training. But that was far from satisfying me. The training of the spirit was possible only through the exercise of the spirit. And the exercise of the spirit entirely depended on the life and character of the teacher. The teacher had always to be mindful of his p s and q s whether he was in the midst of his boys or not.

I saw, therefore, that I must be an eternal object lesson to the boys and girls living with me. They thus became my teachers, and I learnt I must be good and live straight, if only for their sake. I may say that the increasing discipline and restraint I imposed on myself at Tolstoy Farm was mostly due to those wards of mine.

Fasting for a Cause

In those days, I had to move between Johannesburg and Phoenix. Once when I was in Johannesburg I received tidings of the moral fall of two of the inmates of the Ashram. This news came upon me like a thunderbolt. The same day I took the train for Phoenix.

During the journey my duty seemed clear to me. I felt that the guardian or teacher was responsible, to some extent at least, for the lapse of his ward or pupil. My wife had already warned me in the matter, but being of a trusting nature, I had ignored her caution. **I felt that the only way the parties could be made to realize my distress and the depth of their own fall would be for me to do some penance. So I imposed upon myself a fast for seven days and a vow to have only one meal a day for a period of four months and a half.**

My penance pained everybody, but it cleared the atmosphere. Everyone came to realize what a terrible thing it was to be sinful, and the bond that bound me to the boys and girls became stronger and truer. **A circumstance arising out of this incident compelled me a little while after, to go into a fast for fourteen days, the results of which exceeded even my expectations.**[1]

World War One

In 1914, I received Gokhale s instructions to return home via London. So in July Kasturbai, Kallenbach and I sailed for England. On arrival in England I learned that Gokhale had been stranded in Paris where he had gone for reasons of health, and as communication between Paris and London had been cut off, there was no knowing when he would return.

What then was I to do in the meanwhile? What was my duty as regards the war? A meeting of the Indian residents in Great Britain and Ireland was called. I placed my views before them.

I felt that Indians residing in England ought to do their bit in the war. English students had volunteered to serve in the army, and Indians might do no less. A number of objections were taken to this line of argument. There was, it was contended, a world of difference between the Indians and the English. We were slaves and they were masters. How could a slave co-operate with the master in the hour of the latter s need? **Was it not the duty of**

1. Gandhiji used this most unusual method in fighting against the British rulers in India *Ed.*

the slave, seeking to be free to make the master's need his apportunity? This argument failed to appeal to me then. I did not believe that we had been quite reduced to slavery. I felt then that it was more the fault of individual British officials than of the British system, and that we could convert them by love.

I therefore adhered to my advice and invited those who would like to enlist as volunteers. There was a good response, practically all the provinces and all the religions being represented among the volunteers. I wrote a letter to Lord Crewe, acquainting him with these facts and expressing our readiness to be trained for ambulance work, if that should be considered a condition precedent to the acceptance of our offer. He accepted the offer after some hesitation, and thanked us for having tendered our services to the Empire at that critical hour.

The volunteers began their preliminary training in first aid to the wounded under the well-known Dr. Cantlie. It was a short course of six weeks, but it covered the whole course of first aid. We were a class of about 80. In six weeks we were examined, and all except one passed. For these the Government now provided military drill and other training. Colonel Baker was placed in charge of this work.

We were all under the impression that this Commanding Officer was to be our chief only so far as technical matters were concerned, and that in all other matters I was the head of our Corps. But from the first the Officer left us under no such delusion. In a very few days our relations with him reached the breaking point. It was here that an occasion arose for Satyagraha.

I approached the Commanding Officer and drew his attention to the complaints I had received. He wrote asking me to set out the complaints in writing, at the same time asking me to impress upon those who complain that the proper direction in which to make complaints is to me through their section commanders, now appointed, who will inform me through the instructors. To this I replied saying that I had believed that as Chairman of the Volunteer Corps, I should be allowed unofficially to act as their representative.

This did not appeal to the Commanding Officer, who said it was repugnant to all military discipline that the section leaders should be elected by the Corps, and that the recall of appointments already made would be subversive of all discipline. So we held a meeting and decided upon withdrawal. I brought home to the members the serious consequences of Satyagraha. But a very large majority voted for the resolution.

Hereupon I addressed a letter to the Secretary of State for India. He replied explaining that conditions in South Africa were different, and drawing my attention to the fact that under the rules the section commanders were appointed by the Commanding Officer, but assuring me that in future, when appointing section commanders, the Commanding Officer would consider my recommendations.

About this time an unexpectedly large contingent of wounded soldiers arrived at the Netley Hospital, and the services of our Corps were requisitioned. Those whom the Commanding Officer could persuade went to Netley. The others refused to go. Mr. Roberts, the Under-Secretary of State, honoured me with many calls during those days. He insisted on my persuading the others to serve. He suggested that they should form a separate Corps and that at the Netley Hospital they could be responsible only to the Commanding Officer there. This suggestion appealed both to my companions and to me, with the result that those who had stayed away also went to Netley.

Gokhale returned to London soon after, Kallenbach and I used regularly to go to him. Our talks were mostly about the war.

Meanwhile Gokhale left for home, as he could not stand the October fogs of London. Gokhale had inspired a reception for me in Bombay, where he had come in spite of his delicate health.

◆◆◆

Gandhi Flowers

'The best way to find yourself is to lose in the service of others.'

●

9
INDIA AND SATYAGRAHA

Before I reached home, the party which had started from Phoenix had already arrived. They were first put in the Gurukul Kangri, where Swami Shraddhanandji treated them as his own children. After this they were put in the Shantiniketan where the Poet and his people showered similar love upon them.

The receptions in Bombay gave me an occasion for offering what might be called a Little Satyagraha. At the party given in my honour at Mr. Jehangir Petit s place, I did not dare to speak in Gujarati. **In those palatial surroundings of dazzling splendour I, who had lived my best life among indentured labourers, felt myself a complete rustic.** With my Kathiawadi cloak, turban and dhoti, I looked somewhat more civilized than I do today, but the pomp and splendour of Mr. Petit s mansion made me feel absolutely out of my element. However, I acquitted myself tolerably well, having taken shelter under Sir Pherozeshah s protecting wing.

Then there was the Gujarati function which was

·organized by Uttamlal Trivedi. **Mr. Jinnah was present, being a Gujarati. He made a short and sweet little speech in English.** As far as I remember most of the other speeches were also in English. When my turn came, I expressed my thanks in Gujarati explaining my partiality for Gujarati and Hindustani, and entering my humble protest against the use of English in a Gujarati gathering.

The moment I reached Bombay Gokhale sent me word that the Governor was desirous of seeing me, and that it might be proper for me to respond before I left for Poona. Accordingly, I called on His Excellency. After the usual inquiries, he said: I ask one thing of you. **I would like you to come and see me whenever you propose to take any steps connecting Government.'**

I replied: 'I can very easily give the promise, inasmuch as it is my rule, as a Satyagrahi, to understand the viewpoint of the party I propose to deal with, and to try to agree with him as far as may be possible. I strictly observed the rule in South Africa and I mean to do the same here.'

Lord Willingdon thanked me and said: **'You may come to me whenever you like, and you will see that my Government does not wilfully, do anything wrong.**

To which I replied: It is that faith which sustains me.

After this I went to Poona. Gokhale and the members of the Servants of India Society overwhelmed me with affection. I informed Gokhale of my intentions. I wanted to have an Ashram where I could settle down with my Phoenix family, preferably somewhere in Gujarat, Gokhale liked the idea. He said: You should certainly do so. **You must look to me for the expenses of the Ashram, which I will regard as my own.** My heart overflowed with joy. This took a great load off my mind.

From Poona I went to Rajkot and Porbandar, where 1 had to meet my brother s widow and other relatives.

During the Satyagraha in South Africa I had altered my style of dress so as to make it more in keeping with that of the indentured labourers, and in England also I had adhered to the same style for indoor use. For landing in Bombay I had a Kathiawadi suit of clothes, all made of Indian mill cloth. But as I was to travel third from Bombay, I regarded the scarf and the cloak as too much of an incumbrance, so I shed them, and invested in an eight-to-ten annas Kashmiri cap. One dressed in that fashion I was sure to pass muster as a poor man.

My First Satyagraha

On account of the plague prevailing at that time third class passengers were being medically inspected at Viramgam or Wadhwan I forget which. I had slight fever. The inspector on finding that I had a temperature, asked me to report myself to the Medical Officer at Rajkot.

Someone had perhaps sent the information that I was passing through Wadhwan, for the tailor Motilal, a noted public worker of the place, met me at the station. He told me about the Viramgam customs, and the hardships railway passengers had to suffer on account of it. I had little inclination to talk because of my fever, and tried to finish with a brief reply which took the form of a question: 'Are you prepared to go to jail?

He replied with firm deliberation: We will certainly go to jail, provided you lead us.

On reaching Rajkot, I reported myself to the Medical Officer the next morning. I was not unknown there. The doctor felt ashamed and was angry with the inspector.

Wherever I went in Kathiawad I heard complaints about the Viramgam customs and hardships. I therefore decided immediately to make use of Lord Willingdon s offer. I collected and read all the literature available on the subject, convinced myself that the complaints were well-founded, and opened correspondence with the Bombay Government. I called on the Private Secretary to Lord Willingdon and waited on His Excellency also. The latter expressed his sympathy but shifted the blame on Delhi. If it had been in our hands, we should have removed the cordon long ago. You should approach the Government of India, said the Secretary.

I communicated with the Government of India, but got no reply beyond an acknowledgment. It was only when I had an occasion to meet Lord Chelmsford later that redress could be had. When I placed the facts before him, he expressed his astonishment. He had known nothing of the matter. He gave me a patient hearing, telephoned that very moment for papers about Viramgam, and promised to remove the cordon if the authorities had no explanation or defence to offer.

Within a few days of this interview I read in the papers that the Viramgam customs cordon had been removed.

I regarded this event as the advent of Satyagraha in India. For during my interview with the Bombay Government the Secretary had expressed his disapproval of a reference to Satyagraha in a speech which I had delivered in Bagasra.

Is not this a threat? he had asked. And do you think a powerful Government will yield to threats?

This was no threat,' I had replied. It was educating the people. **It is my duty to place before the people all the legitimate remedies for grievances. A nation that wants to come into its own ought to know all the ways and means to freedom. Usually they include violence as the**

last remedy. Satyagraha, on the other hand, is an absolutely non-violent weapon. I regard it as my duty to explain its practice and its limitations. Government is a powerful Government, but I have no doubt also that **Satyagraha is the sovereign remedy.**

The clever Secretary sceptically nodded his head and said: We shall see.

From Rajkot I proceeded to Shantiniketan. The teachers and students overwhelmed me with affection.

I quickly mixed with the teachers and students, and engaged them in a discussion on self-help. I put it to the teachers that, if they and the boys dispensed with the service of paid cooks and cooked their food themselves, it would enable the teachers to control the kitchen from the point of view of the boys physical and moral health, and it would afford to the students an object lesson in self-help. Some of them strongly approved of the proposal. The boys welcomed it, if only because of their instinctive taste for novelty. So we launched the experiment. When I invited the Poet to express his opinion, he said that he did not mind it provided the teachers were favourable. To the boys he said, '**The experiment contains the key to Swaraj.**

I had hardly been there a week when I received from Poona a telegram announcing Gokhale's death. Shantiniketan was immersed in grief. I left for Poona with my wife and Maganlal.

The Satyagraha Ashram was founded on the 25th of May, 1915. When I happened to pass through Ahmedabad, many friends pressed me to settle down there, and they volunteered to fund the expenses of the Ashram, as well as a house for us to live in.

The question of untouchability was naturally among the subjects discussed with the Ahmedabad friends. **I made it clear to them that I should take the first opportunity of admitting an untouchable candidate to the Ashram** if he was otherwise worthy.

The Ashram had been in existence only a few months when I heard from Amritlal Thakkar to this effect: 'A humble and honest untouchable family is desirous of joining your Ashram. Will you accept them?

The family consisted of Dudabhai, his wife Danibehn and their daughter Lakshmi. Dudabhai had been a teacher in Bombay.

But their admission created a flutter amongst the friends who had been helping the Ashram. The very first difficulty was found with regard to the use of the well. The man in charge of the water-lift objected that drops of water from our bucket would pollute him. So he took to swearing at us and molesting Dudabhai. I told everyone to put up with the abuse and continue drawing water at any cost. **When he saw that we did not return his abuse, the man was ashamed and ceased to bother us.**

All monetary help, however, was stopped.

Maganlal Gandhi one day gave me this notice: We are out of funds and there is nothing for the next month.

This was not the first time I had been faced with such a trial. On all such occasions God has sent help at the last moment. One morning, one of the children came and said that a Sheth who was waiting in a car outside wanted to see me. I went out to him. I want to give the Ashram some help. Will you accept it? he asked.

Most certainly, said I. And I confess I am at the present moment at the end of my resources.

Next day, exactly at the appointed hour, the car drew up near our quarters, and the horn was blown. I went out to see him. **He placed in my hands currency notes of the value of Rs. 13,000, and drove away.**

In March 1916 Pandit Madan Mohan Malaviya moved a resolution in the Imperial Legislative Council for the abolition of the indenture system. In accepting the motion Lord Hardinge announced that he had obtained from His Majesty s Government the promise of the abolition in due course of the system. I felt, however, that India could not be satisfied with so very vague an assurance, but ought to agitate for immediate abolition. Might this be a fit subject for Satyagraha? I had no doubt that it was, but I did not know the modus operandi.

It was time for me to tour the country for an all-India agitation. Before I started the agitation I thought it proper to wait upon the Viceroy. So I applied for an interview. He immediately granted it. I had a satisfactory talk with Lord Chelmsford who, without being definite, promised to be helpful.

I began my tour from Bombay. Mr. Jehangir Petit undertook to convene the meeting under the auspices of the Imperial Citizenship Association. The discussion centred round the fixing of the period within which the Government was to be asked to abolish the system. We adopted the 31st July as the latest date.

Mrs. Jaiji Petit put all her energies into the organization of a ladies deputation to the Viceroy. The deputation had a great effect. The Viceroy gave an encouraging reply.

I visited Karachi, Calcutta and various other places. There were fine meetings everywhere, and there was unbounded enthusiasm. Before the 31st July the Government announced that indentured emigration from India was stopped.

Champaran: A Major Satyagraha

Champaran is the land of King Janaka. Just as it abounds in mango groves, so used it to be full of indigo plantations until the year 1917. The Champaran tenant was bound by law to plant three out of every twenty parts of his land with indigo for his landlord.

I had hardly any notion of indigo plantations. I had seen packets of indigo, but little dreamed that it was grown and manufactured in Champaran at great hardship to thousands of agriculturists.

Rajkumar Shukla was one of the agriculturists who was filled with a passion to wash away the stain of indigo for the thousand who were suffering. This man caught hold of me at Lucknow, where I had gone for the Congress of 1916. Vakil Babu will tell you everything about our distress, he said, and urged me to go to Champaran. Vakil Babu was none other than Babu Brajkishore Prasad, who was the soul of public work in Bihar. Rajkumar Shukla brought him to my tent.

So early in 1917, we left Calcutta for Champaran, looking just like fellow rustics. We travelled together, reaching Patna in the morning. Rajkumar Shukla took me to Rajendra Babu s place in Patna. Rajendra Babu had gone to Puri or some other place. There were one or two servants at the bungalow who paid us no attention.

I knew Maulana Mazharul Haq in London when he was studying for the bar, I bethought myself of this invitation and sent him a note indicating the purpose of my visit. He immediately came in his car, and pressed me to accept his hospitality. I requested him to guide me to my destination by the first available train. He suggested that I should first go to Muzaffarpur. There was a train for that place the same evening, and he sent me off by it.

Principal Kripalani was then in Muzaffarpur. I had known of him ever since my visit to Hyderabad. I had sent a telegram informing him of my arrival, and he met me at the station with a crowd of students, though the train reached there at midnight. In the morning a small group of vakils called on me. I still remember Ramnavmi Prasad among them, as his earnestness specially appealed to me.

It is not possible, he said, for you to do the kind of work you have come for, if you stay here. You must come and stay with one of us. Gaya Babu is a well-known vakil here. I have come on his behalf to invite you to stay with him. It is a pity our leaders are not here today. I have, however, wired to them both, Babu Brajkishore Prasad and Babu Rajendra Prasad. I expect them to arrive shortly.

Brajkishore Babu now arrived from Darbhanga and Rajendra Babu from Puri.

Having studied these cases, said I, I have come to the conclusion that we should stop going to law courts. Where the ryots are so crushed and fear-stricken, law courts are useless. I had thought that I should be able to leave here in two days, but I now realize that the work might take even two years. I am prepared to give that time, if necessary.

We sat talking until midnight. I said to them. It may be necessary to face imprisonment, but much as I would love you to run that risk, you would go only so far as you feel yourselves capable of going. I find it difficult to understand the local dialect of Hindi, and I shall not be able to read papers written in Kaithi or Urdu. I shall want you to translate them for me. We cannot afford to pay for this work. It should all be done for love and out of a spirit of service.

They gave me this assurance: The idea of accommodating oneself to imprisonment is a novel thing for us. We will try to assimilate it.

The Secretary of the Planters Association told me plainly that I was an outsider and that I had no business to come between the planters and their tenants, but if I had any representation to make, I might submit it in writing. I politely told him that I did not regard myself as an outsider, and that I had every right to inquire into the condition of the attendants. **The Commissioner, on whom I called, proceeded to bully me, and advised me forthwith to leave Tirhut.**

I acquainted my co-workers with all this, and told them that there was a likelihood of Government stopping me from proceeding further, and that I might have to go to jail earlier than I had expected, it would be best that the arrest should take place in Motihari district headquarters.

I started with my co-workers for Motihari the same day. Babu Gorakh Prasad harboured us in his home, which became a caravanserai. It could hardly contain us all. The very same day we heard that about five miles from Motihari a tenant had been ill-treated. It was decided that I should go and see him the next morning, and we accordingly set off for the place on elephant s back.

We had scarcely gone half way when a messenger from the Police Superintendent overtook us and said that the latter had sent his compliments. I got into the third carriage which the messenger had brought. He then served on me a notice to leave Champaran, and drove me to my place. On his asking me to acknowledge the notice, I wrote to the effect that I did not propose to comply with till my inquiry was finished. Thereupon I received a summons to take my trial the next day for disobeying the order.

The news of the notice and the summons spread like wildfire, and I was told that Motihari that day witnessed unprecedented scenes. The people had for the moment lost all fear of punishment and yielded obedience to the power of love which their new friend exercised.

The trial began. The Government pleader, the Magistrate and other officials were at a loss *to* know what to do. The Government pleader was pressing the Magistrate to postpone the case. But **I interfered and requested the Magistrate not to postpone the case, as I wanted to plead guilty to having disobeyed the order to leave Champaran,** and read a brief statement.

There was now no occasion to postpone the hearing, but as both the Magistrate and the

Government pleader had been taken by surprise, the Magistrate postponed judgment. Meanwhile, I had wired full details to the Viceroy, to Patna friends, and others.

Before I could appear before the court to receive the sentence, the Magistrate sent a written message that the Lieutenant Governor had ordered the case against me to be withdrawn, and the Collector wrote to me saying that I was at liberty to conduct the proposed inquiry, and that I might count on whatever help I needed from the officials. None of us was prepared for this prompt and happy issue.

I called on the Collector Mr. Heycock. He seemed to be a good man, anxious to do justice.

The country thus had its first direct object lesson in Civil Disobedience. The affair was freely discussed both locally and in the press, and my inquiry got unexpected publicity.

The work of recording statements of the ryots grievances was progressing apace. Thousands of such statements were taken, and they could not but have their effect. The ever growing number of ryots coming to make their statements increased the planters wrath, and they moved heaven and earth to counteract my inquiry.

One day I received a letter from the Bihar Government to the following effect: Your inquiry has been sufficiently prolonged, should you not now bring it to an end and leave Bihar?

I wrote in reply that the inquiry was bound to be

prolonged, and unless and until it resulted in bringing relief to the people, I had no intention of leaving Bihar.

Sir Edward Gait, the Lieutenant Governor, asked me to see him, expressed his willingness to appoint an inquiry. Sir Frank Sly was appointed Chairman of the Committee. The Committee found in favour of the ryots, and recommended the *tinkathia* system should be abolished by law.

The *tinkathia* system which had been in existence for about a century was thus abolished, and with it the planters raj came to an end.

Whilst I was yet winding up my work on the Committee, I received a letter from Sjt. Mohanlal Pandya telling me of the failure of crops in the Kheda district, and asking me to guide the peasants, who were unable to pay the assessment.

At the same time there came a letter from Shrimati Anasuyabai about the condition of labour in Ahmedabad. Wages were low, the labourers had long been agitating for an increment, and I had a desire to guide them if I could. So I seized the first opportunity to go to Ahmedabad.

I was in a most delicate situation. Shrimati Anasuyabai had to battle against her own brother, Sjt. Ambalal Sarabhai, who led the fray on behalf of the mill-owners. I had consultations with them, and requested them to refer the dispute to arbitration, but they refused to.

I had therefore to advise the labourers to go on strike. I came in very close contact with them and their leaders, and explained to them the conditions of a successful strike:

1. never to resort to violence,
2. never to molest blacklegs,
3. never to depend upon alms, and
4. to remain firm, no matter how long the strike continued, and to earn bread during the strike, by any other honest labour.

The leaders of the strike understood and accepted the conditions. We had daily meetings of the strikers under the shade of a tree on the bank of the Sabarmati. They daily paraded the streets of the city in peaceful procession. The strike went on for twenty-one days.

A Fast Solved the Problem

For the first two weeks the mill-hands exhibited great courage. But at last they began to show signs of flagging. And I began to fear an outbreak of rowdyism on their part.

One morning it was at a mill-hands meeting while I was still groping and unable to see my way clearly, the light came to me. Unless the strikers rally, I declared to the meeting, and continue the strike till a settlement is reached, or till they leave the mills altogether, I will not touch any food.

In the meantime, Maganlal Gandhi suggested that, as we needed sand for filling the foundation of our weaving school in the Ashram, a number of them might be employed for that purpose. The labourers welcomed the proposal. Anasuyabehn led the way with a basket on her head and soon an endless stream of labourers carrying baskets of sand on their heads could be seen issuing out of the hollow of the river-bed.

Anasuyabehn and a number of other friends and labourers shared the fast with me on the first day. But after some difficulty I was able to dissuade them from continuing it further. The net result of it was that an atmosphere of goodwill was created all round. The hearts of the mill-owners were touched, and they set about discovering some means for a settlement. The strike was called off after I had fasted only for three days. And thus a settlement was reached after 21 days strike.

Kheda Satyagraha

Hardly was the Ahmedabad mill-hands' strike over, when I had to plunge into the Kheda Satyagraha struggle. A condition approaching famine had arisen in the Kheda district owing to a widespered failure of crops, and the Patidars of Kheda were considering the question of getting the revenue assessment for the year suspended. More than one deputation had waited upon the Governor in that connection.

At last I advised the Patidars to resort to Satyagraha. A pledge was signed by the Satyagrahis. The Gujaratis were deeply interested in the fight, which was to them a novel experiment. They were ready to pour forth their riches for the success of the cause, the Bombay merchants sent us more money than necessary, so that we had some balance left at the end of the campaign.

For the Patidar farmers, too, the fight was quite a new thing. We had, therefore, to go about from village to village explaining the principles of Satyagraha. In the initial stages, though the people exhibited much courage, the Government did not seem inclined to take strong action. But as the people s firmness showed no signs of wavering, the Government began coercion. The attachment officers sold people s cattle and seized whatever movables they could lay hand on. Penalty notices were served, and in some cases standing crops were attached.

The campaign came to an unexpected end. The Mamlatdar of the Nadiad Taluka sent me word that, if well-to-do Patidars paid up, the poorer ones would be granted suspension. But as a Mamlatdar could be responsible only for his Taluka, I inquired of the Collector, who alone could give an undertaking in respect of the whole district. He replied that orders declaring suspension in terms of the Mamlatdar s letter had been already issued. I was not aware of it, but if it was a fact, the people s pledge had been fulfilled.

The Kheda Satyagraha marks the beginning of an awakening among the peasants of Gujarat. The lesson was indelibly imprinted on the public mind that the salvation of the people depends upon themselves, upon their capacity for suffering and sacrifice.

The Viceroy had invited various leaders to a war conference in Delhi. I had also been urged to attend the conference. In response to the invitation I went to Delhi. I had, however, objections to taking part in the conference, the principal one being the exclusion from it of leaders like the Ali Brothers. They were then in jail.

I had realized early enough in South Africa that there was no genuine friendship between the Hindus and the Musalmans. I never missed a single opportunity to remove obstacles in the way of unity. It was not in my nature to placate anyone by adulation, or at the cost of self-respect. **But my South African experiences had convinced me that it would be on the question of Hindu-Muslim unity that my Ahimsa would be put to its severest test.**

It was after the imprisonment of the Ali Brothers that I was invited by Muslim friends to attend the session of the Muslim League at Calcutta. Being requested to speak, I addressed them on the duty of the Muslims to secure the Brothers release. A little while after this I was taken by these friends to the Muslim College at Aligarh. **There I invited the young men to be fakirs for the service of the motherland.**

I opened correspondence with the Government for the release of the Brothers. In that connection I studied the Brothers views and activities about the Khilafat. I had discussions with Muslim friends. I felt that, if I would become a true friend of the Muslims, I must render all possible help in securing just settlement of the Khilafat question. It was not for me to enter into the absolute merits of the question, provided there was nothing immoral in their demands. When, therefore, I went to Delhi, I had fully intended to submit the Muslim case to the Viceroy. The Khilafat question had not then assumed the shape it did subsequently.

So I attended the conference. The Viceroy was very keen on my supporting the resolution about recruiting. I asked for permission to speak in Hindi-Hindustani. They Viceroy acceded to my request, but suggested that I should speak also in English. I had no speech to make. I spoke but one sentence to this effect: With a full sense of my responsibility I beg to support the resolution. **Many congratulated me on my having spoken in Hindustani. That was, they said, the first instance within living memory of anyone having spoken in Hindustani at such a meeting.**

I used to issue leaflets asking people to enlist as recruits. Our steady work began to tell. Quite a number of names were registered, and we hoped that we should be able to have a regular supply as soon as the first batch was sent. I had already begun to confer with the Commissioner as to where the recruits were to be accommodated.

First All India Satyagraha

I happened casually to read in the papers the Rowlatt Committee s report which had just been published. Its recommendations startled me. Shankarlal Banker and Umar Sobani approached me with the suggestion that I should take some prompt action in the matter. In about a month I went to Ahmedabad. I mentioned my apprehensions to **Vallabhbhai**, who used to come to see me almost daily. But what can we do in the circumstances? I answered, If even a handful of men can be found to sign the pledge of resistance, and the proposed measure is passed into law in defiance of it, we ought to offer Satyagraha at once.

The proposed conference was held at the Ashram. The Satyagraha pledge was drafted at this meeting, and was signed by all present. I used occasionally to ventilate my views through the daily press. I followed the practice on this occasion. Shankarlal Banker took up the agitation in right earnest. A separate body called the Satyagraha Sabha was established at my instance. Its principal members were drawn from Bombay where, therefore, its headquarters were fixed. The intending conventers began to sign the Satyagraha pledge in large numbers, Bulletins were issued, and popular meetings began to be held everywhere.

The Bill had not yet been gazetted as an Act when I received an invitation from Madras over the signature of Sjt. Kasturi Ranga Iyengar. But the man behind the invitation, was Sjt. **Rajagopalachari**. It was with him that we had put up in Madras. We daily discussed together plans of the fight, **but beyond the holding of public meetings I could not then think of any other programme**.

News was received that the Rowlatt Bill had been published as an Act. That night I fell asleep while thinking over the question. Towards the small hours of the morning I woke up somewhat earlier than usual. I related the whole story to Rajagopalachari: The idea came to me last night in a dream that we should call upon the country to observe a general *hartal*. **Let all the people of India, therefore, suspend their business on that day and observe the day as one of fasting and prayer.** It is very difficult to say whether all the provinces would respond to this appeal of ours or not, but I feel fairly sure of Bombay, Madras, Bihar and Sindh. I think we should have every reason to feel satisfied even if all these places observe the hartal fittingly.'

Rajagopalachari was at once taken up with my suggestion. Other friends too welcomed it when it was communicated to them later. I drafted a brief appeal. The date of the *hartal* was first fixed on the 30th March 1919, but was subsequently changed to 6th April.

Who knows how it all came about? **The whole of India from one end to the other, towns as well as villages, observed a complete hartal on that day. It was a most wonderful spectacle.**

But Delhi had already observed the hartal on the 30th March. The word of Swami Shraddhanandji and Hakim Ajmal Khan Saheb was law there. The wire about the postponement of the hartal had reached there too late. **Delhi had never witnessed a hartal like that before. Hindus and Muslims seemed united like one man. Swami Shraddhanandji was invited to deliver a speech in the Jumma Masjid which he did.** All this was more than the authorities could bear. The police checked the hartal procession as it was proceeding towards the railway station and opened fire, causing a number of casualties, and the reign of repression commencd in Delhi. Shraddhanandji urgently summoned me to Delhi.

The story of the happenings in Delhi was repeated with variations in Lahore and Amritsar. From Amritsar Drs. Satyapal and Kitchlu had sent me a pressing invitation to go there.

The hartal in Bombay was a complete success. It was decided that civil disobedience might be offered in respect of such laws only as easily lent themselves to being disobeyed by the masses. The salt tax was extremely unpopular and a powerful movement had been for some time past going on to secure its repeal. **I therefore suggested that the people might prepare salt from sea-water in their own houses in disregard of the salt laws. My other suggestions, was about the sale of proscribed**

literature. Two of my books, *Hind Swaraj* and *Sarvodaya* which had been already proscribed, came handy for this purpose.

On the evening of the 6th an army of volunteers issued forth accordingly with this prohibited literature to sell it among the people. Both Sarojini Devi and I went out in cars. All the copies were soon sold out. Both these books were priced at four annas per copy, but quite a large number of people simply poured out all the cash that was in their pockets to purchase their copy. It was duly explained to the people that they were liable to be arrested and imprisoned for purchasing the proscribed literature. But for the moment they has shed all fear of jail-going.

Arrest at Palwal

On the night of the 7th I started for Delhi and Amritsar. On reaching Mathura on the 8th I first heard rumours about my probable arrest. **Before the train had reached Palwal railway station, I was served with a written order to the effect that I was prohibited from entering the boundary of Punjab**, as my presence there was likely to result in disturbance of the peace. I was asked by the police to get down from the train. I refused to do so saying, 'I want to go to Punjab in response to a pressing invitation, not to foment unrest, but to allay it.

At Palwal railway station I was taken out of the train and put under police custody. A train from Delhi came in a short time. I was made to enter a third class carriage. On reaching Mathura, I was taken to the police barracks. **Early at 4 o clock the next morning I was woken up and put in a goods train that was going towards Bombay.** At noon I was again made to get down at Sawai Madhopur. Mr. Bowring, Inspector of Police, who arrived by the mail train from Lahore, now took charge of me. I was put in a first class compartment with him.

He requested me to return to Bombay of my own accord and agree not to cross the frontier of Punjab. I replied that I could not possibly comply with the order, and that I was not prepared of my own accord to go back. Whereupon the officer told me that he would have to enforce the law against me. But what do you want to do with me? He replied that he himself did not know, but was awaiting further orders. For the present, he said, I am taking you to Bombay.

We reached Surat. Here I was made over to the charge of another police officer. You are now free, the officer told me when we had reached Bombay. It would however be better, he added, if you get down near the Marine Lines where I shall get the train stopped for you. At Colaba there is likely to be a big crowd. Accordingly. I alighted at the Marine Lines. The carriage of a friend just happened to be passing by. It took me and left me at Revashankar Jhaveri s place. The friend told me that **the news**

of my arrest had incensed the people and roused them to a pitch of mad frenzy. An outbreak is apprehended every minute near Pydhuni.

Umar Sobani and Anasuyabehn arrived and asked me to motor to Pydhuni at once. The people have become impatient, and are very much excited, they said, we cannot pacify them. Your presence alone can do it.

At Pydhuni we sighted a body of mounted police. Brickbats were raining down from above. I besought the crowd to be calm. As the procession issued out of Abdur Rahman Street and was about to proceed towards the Crawford Market, it suddenly found itself confronted by a body of the mounted police.

There was hardly any chance of my voice being heard in that vast concourse. Just then the officer in charge gave the order to disperse the crowd, and at once the mounted party charged upon the crowd brandishing their lances as they went. The ranks of the people were soon broken, and they were thrown into utter confusion. Some got trampled under foot, others were badly mauled and crushed.

Thus the crowd was dispersed and its progress checked. Our motor was allowed to proceed. I had it stopped before the Commissioner s office, and got down to complain to him about the conduct of the police.

When I was admitted to the office, I saw Mr. Bowring sitting with Mr. Griffith. I described to the Commissioner the scenes I had witnessed. He replied briefly: I did not want the procession to proceed to the Fort. And as I saw that the people would not listen to persuasion, I could not help ordering the mounted police to charge through the crowd.

But, said I, 'you knew what the consequences must be. The horses were bound to trample on the people. I think it was quite unnecessary to send that contingent of mounted men.

'You cannot judge that, said Mr. Griffith. We police officers know better than you the effect of your teaching on the people. I have no doubt about your intentions, but the people will not understand them. They will follow their natural instinct.

It is there that I join issue with you, I replied. The people are not by nature violent but peaceful.

And thus we argued at length. It was impossible for us to agree. I told him that I intended to address a meeting at Chaupati and to ask the people to keep the peace, and took leave of him.

I proceeded to Ahmedabad. I learnt that an attempt had been made to pull up the rails near the Nadiad railway station, that **a Government officer had been murdered in Viramgam and that Ahmedabad was under martial law.**

A police officer was waiting at the station to escort me to Mr. Pratt, the Commissioner. I found him in a state of rage. I spoke to him gently, and expressed my regret for the disturbances. I declared my readiness to co-operate in all efforts to restore peace. I asked for permission to hold a public meeting on the grounds of the Sabarmati Ashram. The proposal appealed to him, and the meeting was held, and martial law was withdrawn the same day or the day after. Addressing the meeting, I tried to bring home to the people the sense of their wrong, **declared a penitential fast of three days for myself, appealed to the people to go on a similar fast for a day,** and suggested to those who had been guilty of acts of violence to confess their guilt.

Ramanbhai and other citizens of Ahmedabad came to me with an appeal to suspend the Satyagraha. **I had already made up my mind to suspend the Satyagraha so long as people had not learnt the lesson of peace.** The friends went away happy.

Government s policy of lawless repression was in full course and was manifesting itself in the Punjab in all its nakedness. Leaders were put under arrest, martial law, which in other words meant no law, was proclaimed, special tribunals were set up. Sentences were passed unwarranted by evidence and in flagrant violation of justice. In Amritsar innocent men and women were made to crawl like worms on their bellies. Before this outrage the Jalianwala Bagh tragedy paled into insignificance in my eyes, though it was this massacre principally that attracted the attention of the people of India and the world.

In the meantime, the Hunter Committee was announced to hold an inquiry in connection with the Punjab Government s doings under the martial law. I once more telegraphed to the Viceroy asking whether I could now go to Punjab. He wired back in reply that I could go there after a certain date.

The scene that I witnessed on my arrival at Lahore can never be effaced from my memory. **The railway station was from end to end one seething mass of humanity.** I was put up at Pandit Rambhaj Dutt's bungalow. Owing to the principal Punjab leaders being in jail, their place, I found, had been properly taken up by Pandit Malaviyaji, Pandit Motilalji and Swami Shraddhanandji.

It was decided to appoint a non-official Inquiry Committee to hold almost a parallel inquiry on behalf of the Congress. Deshbandhu C.R. Das, Sjt. Abbas Tyabji, Sjt. M.R. Jayakar and myself were appointed to this Committee virtually by Pandit Malaviyaji. We distributed ourselves over various places for the purpose of inquiry. The responsibility for organizing the work of the Committee devovled on me.

The task of drafting the report of this was also entrusted to me. This report will enable the reader to see to what lengths the British Government is capable of going, and what inhumanities and barbarities it is capable of perpetrating in order to maintain its power. So far as I am aware, not a single statement made in this report has ever been disproved.

The Congress inquiry had just commenced, when I received a letter of invitation to be present at a joint conference of Hindus and Muslmins that was to meet at Delhi to deliberate on the Khilafat question. The letter went on to say, that the question of cow protection as well would be discussed. I did not like this reference. In my letter in reply I suggested that the two questions should not be mixed up together or considered in the spirit of a bargain, but should be decided on their own merits and treated separately. Before the conference I contended that, if the Khilafat question had a just and legitimate basis, as I believe it had, and if the Government had really committed a gross injustice, the Hindus were bound to stand by the Muslims in their demand for the redress of the Khilafat wrong.

Maulana Abdul Bari Saheb said: No matter whether the Hindus help us or not, the Muslims ought, as the countrymen of the Hindus, out of regard for the latter s susceptibilities, to give up cow slaughter. And at one time it almost looked as if they would really put an end to it.

Among the numerous resolutions that were passed at this conference, **one called upon both Hindus and Muslims to take the Swadeshi vow, and as a natural corollary to it, to boycott foreign goods.**

Amritsar Congress

The Punjab Government could not keep in confinement the hundreds of Punjabis who, under the martial law regime, had been clapped into jail. Most of the prisoners were released before the Amritsar Congress opened. Lala Harkishanlal and the other leaders were all released while the session of the Congress was still in progress. The Ali Brothers too arrived there straight from jail. Pandit Motilal Nehru, who, at the sacrifice of his splendid practice, had made Punjab his headquarters and had done great service, was the President of the Congress; Swami Shraddhanandji was the Chairman of the Reception Committee.

Pandit Malaviyaji had harboured me in his own room. I was able to observe his daily routine in the closest detail. His room presented the appearance of a free inn for all the poor. You could hardly cross from one end to the other. In a corner of this crib lay my *charpai* in all its dignity.

I must regard my participation in Congress proceedings at Amritsar as my real entrance into the Congress politics. My experience had shown that there were one or two things for which perhaps I had some aptitude and which could be useful to the Congress. I could already see that Lokmanya, Deshabandhu, Pandit Motilalji and other leaders were pleased with my work in connection with the Punjab inquiry.

My other aptitude which the Congress could utilize was as a draftsman. The Congress

leaders had found that I had a faculty for condensed expression. The then existing constitution of the Congress was Gokhale's legacy. He had framed a few rules which served as the basis for running the Congress machinery. But everybody had now come to feel that these rules were no longer adequate for the ever increasing business of the Congress.

I undertook the responsibility of framing a constitution on one condition. I saw that there were two leaders, Lokmanya and Deshabandhu who had the greatest hold on the public. I requested that they should be associated with me on the Committee. But since it was obvious that they would not have the time personally to participate in the work, I suggested that two persons enjoying their confidence should be appointed along with me. This suggestion was accepted by Lokmanya and Deshabandhu, who suggested the names of Sjts. Kelkar and I. B. Sen respectively as their proxies.

The Committee could not even once come together, but we were able to consult with each other by correspondence, and in the end presented a unanimous report. I regard this constitution with a certain measure of pride. I hold that, if we could fully work out this constitution, the mere fact of working it out would bring us Swaraj. With the assumption of this responsibility I may be said to have made my real entrance into the Congress politics.

The Khadi Story

I do not remember to have seen a handloom or a spinning wheel when in 1908 I described it in *Hind Swaraj* as the panacea for the growing pauperism of India. When the Satyagraha Ashram was founded at Sabarmati, we introduced a few handlooms there. We needed a weaving expert to teach us to weave before we could work the looms. One was at last procured from Palanpur.

We discarded the use of mill-woven cloth, and all the members of the Ashram resolved to wear handwoven cloth made from Indian yarn only. The adoption of this practice brought us a world of experience. It enabled us to know, from direct contact, the conditions of life among the weavers, and the extent of their production. We were not in a position immediately to manufacture all the cloth for our needs. The alternative was to get our cloth supply from handloom weavers. But readymade cloth from Indian mill-yarn was not easily obtainable. All the fine cloth woven by the weavers was from foreign yarn, since Indian mills did not spin fine counts.

So the time passed on, and my impatience grew with the time. I plied every chance visitor to the Ashram who was likely to possess some information about handspinning. But the art being confined to women and having been all but exterminated, if there was some stray spinner still surviving in some obscure corner, only a member of that sex was likely to find out her whereabouts.

In the year 1917 I was taken by my Gujarati friends to preside at the Broach Educational Conference. It was here that I discovered that remarkable lady Gangabehn Majmudar. She was a widow, but her enterprising spirit knew no bounds. She had a well seasoned constitution, and went about everywhere without an escort. She felt quite at home on horseback. To her I poured out my grief about the charkha, and she lightened my burden by a promise to prosecute an earnest and incessant search for the spinning wheel.

At last, after no end of wandering in Gujarat, Gangabehn found the spinning wheel in Vijapur in the Baroda State. Quite a number of people there had spinning wheels in their homes, but had long since consigned them to the lofts as useless lumber. They expressed to Gangabehn their readiness to resume spinning if someone promised to provide them with a regular supply of slivers, and to buy the yarn spun by them. Gangabehn communicated the joyful news to me. I sent to Gangabehn the slivers, and soon yarn began to pour in at such a rate that it became quite a problem how to cope with it.

The spinning wheel gained a rapid footing in the Ashram. The first piece of Khadi manufactured in the Ashram cost 17 annas per yard.

I now grew impatient for the exclusive adoption of Khadi for my dress. My *dhoti* was still of Indian mill cloth. The coarse Khadi manufactured in the Ashram and at Vijapur was only 30 inches in width. I gave notice to Gangabehn that, unless she provided me with a Khadi *dhoti* of 45 inches width within a month, I would do with coarse, short Khadi *dhoti*. The ultimatum came upon her as a shock. But she proved equal to the demand made upon her. Well within the month she sent me a pair of Khadi *dhotis* of 45 inches width.

At about the same time Sjt. Lakshmidas brought Sjt. Ramji, the weaver, with his wife from Lathi to the Ashram and got Khadi *dhotis* woven at the Ashram. The part played by this couple in the spread of Khadi was by no means insignificant.

Non-Violent Non-Cooperation

Whilst the powerful Khilafat agitation set up by the Ali Brothers was in full progress, I had long discussions on the subject with Maulana Abdul Bari and the other Ulema, especially, with regard to the extent to which a Muslim could observe the rule of non-violence. In the end **they all agreed that Islam did not forbid its followers from following non-violence as a policy, and further, that they were bound faithfully to carry it out.** At last the non-cooperation resolution was moved in the Khilafat Conference, and carried after prolonged deliberations. Next, the non-cooperation resolution